HORRINGER COURT MIDDLE SCHOOL
GLASTONBURY ROAD,
BURY ST. EDMUNDS,
IP33 2EX.

CAMPFIRE TALES OF THE AMERICAN INDIANS

Magic is the word for these stories of heroes and heroines, of ghosts and monsters, of humour, mystery and daring deeds. Around campfires, in tepees or wigwams, the tale spinners tried to make their listeners shake with laughter, shiver with terror or sit breathless with suspense. Only stories that held their audiences survived the oral tradition. The best of these drawn from the earliest recorded folk material of more than two dozen American Indian tribes are included in this collection, all being retold by Dee Brown as they would be related by a tale teller of today.

By the same Author

★

WOUNDED KNEE
Abridged edition of *Bury My Heart At Wounded Knee*

BURY MY HEART AT WOUNDED KNEE
An Indian History of the American West

HEAR THAT LONESOME WHISTLE BLOW
Railroads in the American West

CAMPFIRE TALES OF THE AMERICAN INDIANS

Retold for Our Times

by

DEE BROWN

With illustrations by
LOUIS MOFSIE

1979
CHATTO & WINDUS
LONDON

Published by
Chatto & Windus Ltd.
40–42 William IV Street
London WC2N 4DF

In order to publish this book at the lowest possible price, the same text has been used in both British and American editions. For this reason, American spellings such as honor (for British honour), traveled (for travelled) and center (for centre) will be found throughout the book.

All rights reserved. No part of this publication may be reproduced, stored in a retrieval system, or transmitted in any form, or by any means, electronic, mechanical, photocopying, recording or otherwise, without the prior permission of Chatto & Windus Ltd.

© 1979 by Dee Brown
Illustrations ©1979 by Louis Mofsie
First edition 1979

ISBN 0 7011 2354 0

Printed in Great Britain by
Ebenezer Baylis and Son Limited
The Trinity Press, Worcester, and London

For the pleasure of
Nicholas Brave Wolf & Friends

CONTENTS

	page
INTRODUCTION	9
I WHEN ANIMALS LIVED AS EQUALS WITH THE PEOPLE	11
The Rooster, the Mockingbird and the Maiden (Hopi)	14
The Bear Man (Cherokee)	18
How Antelope Carrier Saved the Thunderbirds (Arikara)	22
Why Dogs Have Long Tongues (Caddo)	26
✓ The Great Shell of Kintyel (Navaho)	28
The Girl Who Climbed to the Sky (Arapaho-Caddo)	39
II BEFORE THE WHITE MEN CAME	43
The Cheyenne Prophet (Cheyenne)	46
The Deeds and Prophecies of Old Man (Blackfoot)	59
✓ How Day and Night Were Divided (Creek)	62
✓ How the Buffalo Were Released on Earth (Apache–Comanche)	63
✓ How Corn Came to the Earth (Arikara)	65
✓ How Rabbit Brought Fire to the People (Creek)	70
Godasiyo the Woman Chief (Seneca)	71
III ALLEGORIES	75
The Return of Ice Man (Cherokee)	78
Ice Man and the Messenger of Springtime (Chippewa)	79
IV FIRST CONTACTS WITH EUROPEANS	81
How Ioscoda and His Friends Met the White Men from the East and Journeyed Across the Great Waters (Ottawa)	84
Katlian and the Iron People (Tlingit)	90
✓ How the First White Men Came to the Cheyennes (Cheyenne)	92

V	THE COMING OF THE HORSE	95
	How a Piegan Warrior Found the First Horses (Blackfoot)	98
	Water Spirit's Gift of Horses (Blackfoot)	99
VI	TRICKSTERS AND MAGICIANS	103
	How Rabbit Fooled Wolf (Creek)	106
	Coyote and the Rolling Rock (Salish-Blackfoot)	109
	Skunk Outwits Coyote (Comanche)	111
	Nihancan and the Dwarf's Arrow (Arapaho)	114
	Swift-Runner and the Trickster Tarantula (Zuni)	115
	Buffalo Woman, A Story of Magic (Caddo)	123
VII	HEROES AND HEROINES	129
	The Hunter and the Dakwa (Cherokee)	132
	The Prisoners of Court House Rock (Pawnee)	133
	Red Shield and Running Wolf (Crow)	135
VIII	ANIMAL STORIES	143
	The Bluebird and the Coyote (Pima)	146
	The Story of the Bat (Creek)	147
	Crow and Hawk (Cochiti)	148
	Why Coyote Stopped Imitating His Friends (Caddo)	150
IX	GHOST STORIES	155
	The Lame Warrior and the Skeleton (Arapaho)	158
	Heavy Collar and the Ghost Woman (Blackfoot)	160
	The Sioux Who Wrestled With A Ghost (Sioux)	166
SOURCES		169

INTRODUCTION

Had it not been for a few far-sighted anthropologists, ethnologists, folklorists, and non-professional lovers of good stories who wanted to make a permanent record of the traditions of American Indians, we would now have almost no legends and tales of these people. Around the end of the nineteenth century and the beginning of the twentieth, these dedicated collectors realized that hundreds of Indian tales which had been passed orally through the centuries from storyteller to storyteller would be lost forever unless someone wrote them down.

Among those who devoted years of their lifetimes to this task were George A. Dorsey, George B. Grinnell, James Mooney, Alfred L. Kroeber, Robert H. Lowie, John R. Swanton, William O. Tuggle, Ruth Benedict, Louise McDermott, Henry Schoolcraft, Clark Wissler, Frank Hamilton Cushing, Washington Matthews, and several others whose work is included in this collection. Working independently or supported by organizations such as the U.S. Bureau of American Ethnology, the Carnegie Institution of Washington, the American Museum of Natural History, the American Folklore Society, and the Field Columbian Museum of Chicago, they went to Indian reservations and villages and won the confidence of the last of the old tale tellers of the various tribes.

What I have looked for in the records they saved for us are tales of adventure and heroism, of quests and accomplishments, of mystery and suspense, of magic and trickery, of ghosts and monsters. Many of the stories were chosen because they are sprinkled with those delightful touches of fun and good humor that are characteristic of American Indians.

Readers unfamiliar with Indian stories will find that the food, shelter, clothing, animals, and geographical settings are different from those they are accustomed to in tales of other peoples. Yet basically the stories deal with the same strengths and weaknesses of human beings everywhere. The situations are universal, reminiscent of life as it goes on anywhere on this earth.

Most of the original narratives were taken down, often through interpreters, exactly as they were told many years ago and mainly for the use of other scholars. Because the language was sometimes archaic, the incidents disconnected, the plots and meanings often obscure, I have retold most of them as I believe they would be told by an English-speaking American Indian tale teller of today.

Years ago when Dr. Washington Matthews published his Navaho legends, he invited "poets, novelists, travellers, and compilers" to search his book and cull from it whatever facts and fancies they might choose. His only requests were that they would not garble or distort what he had written, nor put alien thoughts into the minds of his heroes, nor arm them with weapons or clothe them in the habiliments of an alien race, nor make them act incongruous parts. As best I could I have followed Dr. Matthews' commandments, and I pray that I have at least partially succeeded.

DEE BROWN

I

When Animals Lived as Equals with the People

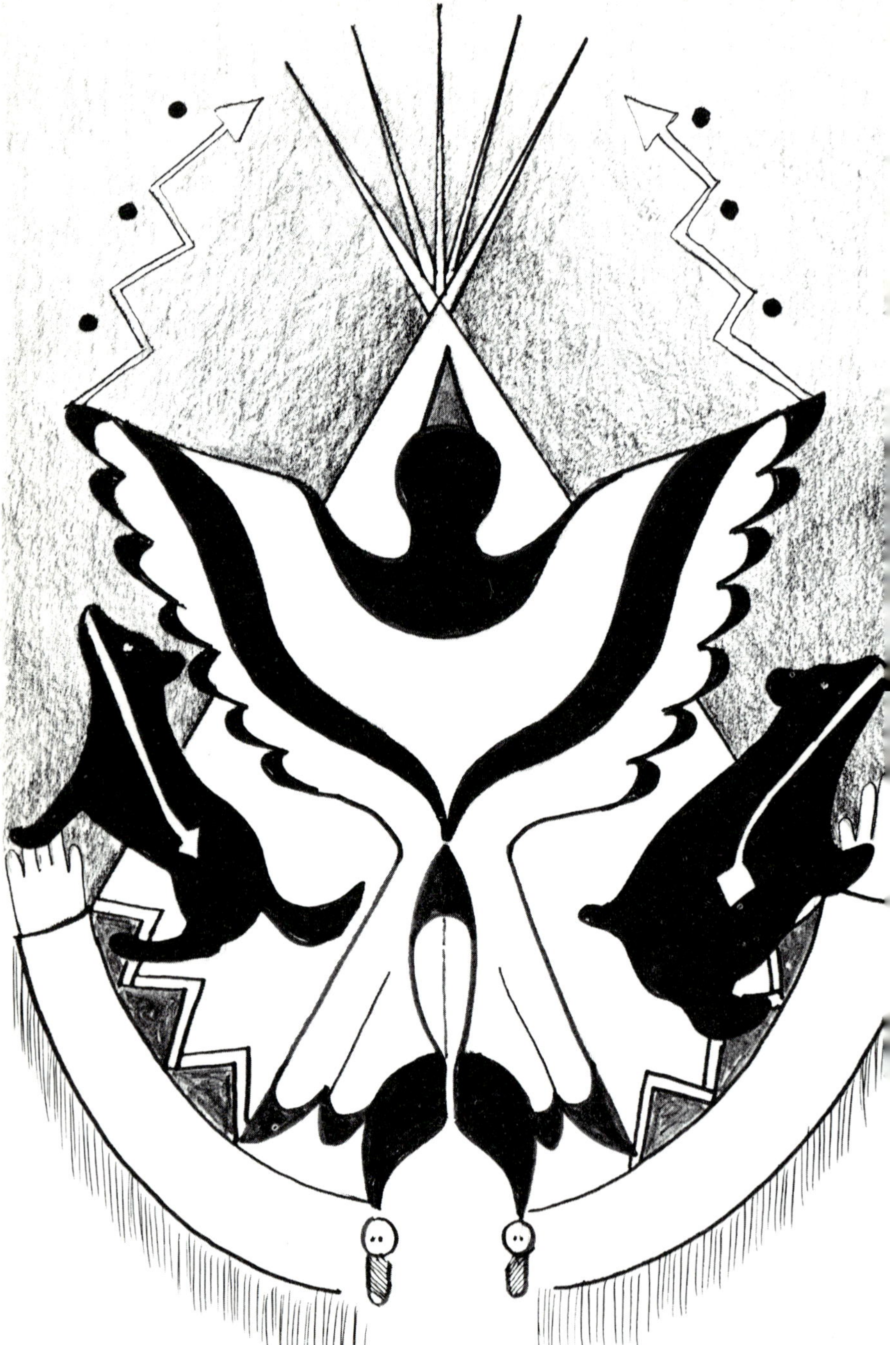

In the myths of some American Indian tribes, the first animals on earth were equals with human beings in size and intelligence, speaking their language and often assuming the forms of people. For some unknown reason the first animals vanished and were replaced by those we now know.

In these six representative tales, we find humor and tragedy, heroes, heroines, and villains, a fable and a rite-myth—with animals playing roles fully equal to human beings.

The Rooster, the Mockingbird and the Maiden
(Hopi)

In the old days many Hopis lived at Oraibi, with birds and animals living as equals among them. At the northwest part of Bakvatovi pueblo lived a beautiful maiden who persistently refused all offers of marriage. The young men of Oraibi brought gifts to her, hoping to win her as a wife, but she returned their presents and sent them away.

Far away to the north a powerful chief heard of her beauty and made the long journey to Oraibi to win her consent to marry. He brought with him a bundle of presents, which he set down outside her house before entering to introduce himself. He found the girl grinding cornmeal.

Without stopping her work, she looked up at the handsome visitor, but said nothing.

"Why do you not talk to me?" he asked.

"Who are you, going around here?" she replied.

"I came to ask you to marry me," he said. "I left my bundle of gifts outside. Go and look at them."

The girl stopped her grinding, went outside, and found a large basket woven of bright yellow reeds. She brought it into the house, and opening it found two yellow bridal robes, a pair of yellow moccasins, and a wide yellow belt. After looking at the gifts for a moment, she put them back into the basket and handed it to the young chief. "I do not want them," she said. "I do not want you. You may go now."

The young man bowed his head, picked up the basket, and left.

Now, over on another side of Oraibi lived a Rooster, a very proud Rooster, who could assume the appearance of a man whenever he chose to do so. That afternoon he heard about the visit of the chief from the north, and he thought it strange that this beautiful maiden had sent the powerful chief away. So curious was he that he made preparations to visit her that very evening. Changing himself into a handsome youth, the Rooster dressed in a red shirt figured with black lines. He also wore turquoise ear pendants, and on top of his head a bunch of red feathers. When he went up into the girl's house he found her drying cornmeal in a pot over a fire, and he could tell at once that she was pleased by his appearance.

The Rooster acted like a perfect gentleman, seating himself by the side of the fireplace and complimenting her on the fine art objects she had assembled in the room. Pleased by his remarks, the girl began chatting merrily with him. When he arose and boldly asked her to marry him, the girl told him to return in four days and she would do so.

Being a very proud Rooster, he was not surprised that the girl had accepted him instead of sending him away as she had all her other suitors. "Very well," he said, "I shall return in four days."

Now, there was a Mockingbird who lived in a peach orchard somewhat south of that pueblo. On the third day after the Rooster visited the beautiful girl, the Mockingbird heard about it. This Mockingbird was a strong rival of the Rooster, and he was extremely provoked to learn that the girl had agreed to marry him. Like the Rooster, the Mockingbird possessed the power to change himself into a man. He did so immediately, dressed himself splendidly, and hurried over to visit the maiden. He had made himself so handsome, and his voice was so musical that the girl was quite bewitched by him. She went to tell her mother that she had changed her mind. She would marry the Mockingbird instead of the Rooster. "Very well," her mother said, "if you think you can trust him."

Meanwhile the Rooster, who had grown so enamored of the girl that he spent most of his time watching her house in hopes of catching a glimpse of her, happened to see the Mockingbird go up to the pueblo Bakvatovi. After a while the Rooster's curiosity turned to jealousy and he ran up to the door of the girl's house and knocked. Without waiting to be admitted, he entered and found the Mockingbird sitting by the fireplace. "What are you doing here?" he shouted at the Mockingbird.

"I have come to marry this maiden," the Mockingbird replied.

"Not so," the Rooster said. "Tomorrow it is I who shall marry her. You are not worthy of her. I own all these people here in

Oraibi. They are mine. When I crow in the morning they all get up."

"I am worth more than you," retorted the Mockingbird. "When I twitter and sing in the morning I make the sun come up."

"Very well," the Rooster said. "Let us compete with each other and see who is worth the most. In three days we shall have a contest and see who can make the sun rise. Until then no one shall marry the maiden."

The Mockingbird agreed and they both left the girl's house. When the Rooster returned home he sat down and thought of how he could beat the Mockingbird by making the sun rise. He knew there was no use asking for help from the god of the eagle clan, the Great Thunderbird, because he favored Mockingbirds. Finally the Rooster decided to go to Moenkopi and ask the wisest of the Roosters and Hens who lived there to teach him how to make the sun rise.

It was a long distance to Moenkopi, and by the time the Rooster reached Bow Mound he was so weary that he feared he could go no farther. He sat down on a stone beside a *paho* shrine to rest, and when he did so an opening appeared in the shrine and he heard a voice say: "Come in." He entered and was greeted by several beautiful girls, one of whom brought him a tray of shelled corn. He picked and ate it like Roosters eat, and when he was no longer hungry, the girl said: "You were tired from running so far. Now you have the strength to reach your destination." The Rooster thanked the girls and went out. Feeling somewhat revived, he continued his journey, running very fast until he reached Moenkopi.

There he came to a steep bluff which he descended by a ladder to a large rock with an opening closed by a heavy door. The Rooster crowed repeatedly until the door was opened and a voice invited him to enter. Inside he found many Roosters and Hens of all ages. They seemed pleased that he had come to see them, offered him a place to sit, and brought him some shelled corn.

"What circumstance brings you to honor us with your presence?" the chief Rooster asked politely.

"At Oraibi a Mockingbird and I are contending over a maiden," the Rooster replied. "We are contesting to see which of us has the most power. When I crow in the morning all the people get up, but when the Mockingbird sings the sun comes up. I want you to teach me how to make the sun rise and bring light to the world."

"Very well," the Rooster chief said. "We shall at least try. The Mockingbird is very powerful and he has the help of the Great Thunderbird, but we shall at least try."

When evening came the Roosters and Hens gathered and sang into the night. After they finished singing four long songs the Roosters all crowed. Then they sang four more songs, and crowed again. After singing three more songs they crowed a third time. By now the yellow dawn was appearing, and after they sang two more songs, the sun rose above the rim of the earth.

"We have done what needed to be done," the chief Rooster said. "Now you can go home and show the Mockingbird that you can make the sun come up."

The Rooster started back to Oraibi, running very fast. Again, when he reached Bow Mound he fell exhausted by the *paho* shrine and went inside. "I am too worn out to run any farther," he said to the girls. "I shall never get home in time." They laughed at him and brought him some shelled corn. "Of course you will get home in time," they assured him. "We shall dress you up and then you will get home in time." While he was eating they stood behind him so he could not see them fastening dry corn husks to his tail feathers.

When he started running toward Oraibi, the corn husks rattled loudly. He was so frightened by the rattling that he ran very fast, never looking back, all the way to his house. When he went inside, he found the corn husks on his tail and removed them.

He rested all night and the next morning he felt very strong. Late in the day he walked through the pueblo to the peach orchard where the Mockingbird lived and told him to come over to his house that night for the contest. After the Rooster left, the Mockingbird went to see the Great Thunderbird and informed him that the time had come to prove his power over the sun.

That evening the Mockingbird came to the Rooster's house to await the next dawn. All through the night the Rooster sang and crowed until the first yellow of daylight appeared. Then he finished the last two songs he had learned at Moenkopi and began crowing with all his might. About this time, however, the Great Thunderbird flew up and spread his large wings across the eastern sky, completely covering up the dawn. No matter how loud the Rooster crowed, the sun did not hear him and would not rise. The Mockingbird laughed at the Rooster. "You have failed," he said. "Now it is my turn. Come to my house tonight and I will show you how it is done."

That evening the Rooster went to the Mockingbird's house. After darkness fell the Mockingbird sang four long songs and then whistled. He waited a while and sang three more songs and whistled, and the dawn began to appear. He then sang his last two songs, and very slowly the sun rose above the rim of the earth. "You see," the Mockingbird cried triumphantly, "only I can make the sun come up."

"Yes," the Rooster admitted, "you have great powers. You know how to make the sun rise. You have won the Bakvatovi maiden for your wife."

And so the Mockingbird married the beautiful girl. Later on, the Rooster also found himself a wife, one not nearly so beautiful. By and by children were born. Those of the Mockingbird talked and jabbered constantly like their father, but the children of the Rooster were kind and gentle and did not talk so much.

The Bear Man

(Cherokee)

One springtime morning a Cherokee named Whirlwind told his wife goodbye and left his village to go up in the Smoky Mountains to hunt for wild game. In the forest he saw a black bear and wounded it with an arrow. The bear turned and started to run away, but the hunter followed, shooting one arrow after another into the animal without bringing it down. Whirlwind did not know that this bear possessed secret powers, and could talk and read the thoughts of people.

At last the black bear stopped and pulled the arrows out of his body and gave them to Whirlwind. "It is of no use for you to shoot at me," he said. "You can't kill me. Come with me and I will show you how bears live."

"This bear may kill me," Whirlwind said to himself, but the bear read his thoughts and said: "No, I will not hurt you."

"How can I get anything to eat if I go with this bear?" Whirlwind thought, and again the bear knew what the hunter was thinking, and said: "I have plenty of food."

Whirlwind decided to go with the bear. They walked until they came to a cave in the side of a mountain, and the bear said: "This is not where I live, but we are holding a council here and you can see what we do." They entered the cave, which widened as they went farther in until it was as large as a Cherokee townhouse. It was filled with bears, old and young, brown and black, and one large white bear who was the chief. Whirlwind sat down in a corner beside the black bear who had brought him inside, but soon the other bears scented his presence.

"What is that bad smell of a man?" one asked, but the bear chief answered: "Don't talk so. It is only a stranger come to see us. Let him alone."

The bears began to talk among themselves, and Whirlwind was astonished that he could understand what they were saying. They were discussing the scarcity of food of all kinds in the mountains, and were trying to decide what to do about it. They had sent messengers in all directions, and two of them had returned to report on what they had found. In a valley to the south, they said, was a large stand of chestnuts and oaks, and the ground beneath them was covered with mast. Pleased at this news, a huge black bear named Long Hams announced that he would lead them in a dance.

While they were dancing, the bears noticed Whirlwind's bow and arrows, and Long Hams stopped and said: "This is what men use to kill us. Let us see if we can use them. Maybe we can fight them with their own weapons."

Long Hams took the bow and arrows from Whirlwind. He fitted an arrow and drew back the sinew string, but when he let go, the string caught in his long claws and the arrow fell to the ground. He saw that he could not use the bow and arrows and gave them back to Whirlwind. By this time, the bears had finished their dance, and were leaving the cave to go to their separate homes.

Whirlwind went out with the black bear who had brought him there, and after a long walk they came to a smaller cave in the side of the mountain. "This is where I live," the bear said, and led the way inside. Whirlwind could see no food anywhere in the cave, and wondered how he was going to get something to satisfy his hunger. Reading his thoughts, the bear sat up on his hind legs and made a movement with his forepaws. When he held his paws out to Whirlwind they were filled with chestnuts. He repeated this magic and his paws were filled with huckleberries which he gave to Whirlwind. He then presented him with blackberries, and finally some acorns.

"I cannot eat acorns," Whirlwind said. "Besides you have given me enough to eat already."

For many moons, through the summer and winter, Whirlwind lived in the cave with the bear. After a while he noticed that his hair was growing all over his body like that of a bear. He learned to eat acorns and act like a bear, but he still walked upright like a man.

On the first warm day of spring the bear told Whirlwind that he had dreamed of the Cherokee village down in the valley. In the dream he heard the Cherokees talking of a big hunt in the mountains.

"Is my wife still there waiting for me?" Whirlwind asked.

"She awaits your return," the bear replied. "But you have become a bear man. If you return you must shut yourself out of sight of your people for seven days without food or drink. At the end of that time you will become like a man again."

A few days later a party of Cherokee hunters came up into the mountains. The black bear and Whirlwind hid themselves in the cave, but the hunters' dogs found the entrance and began to bark furiously.

"I have lost my power against arrows," the bear said. "Your people will kill me and take my skin from me, but they will not harm you. They will take you home with them. Remember what I told you, if you wish to lose your bear nature and become a man again."

The Cherokee hunters began throwing lighted pine knots inside the cave.

"They will kill me and drag me outside and cut me in pieces," the bear said. "Afterwards you must cover my blood with leaves. When they are taking you away, if you look back you will see something."

As the bear had foretold, the hunters killed him with arrows and dragged his body outside and took the skin from it and cut the meat into quarters to carry back to their village. Fearing that they might mistake him for another bear, Whirlwind remained in the cave, but the dogs continued barking at him. When the hunters looked inside they saw a hairy man standing upright, and one of them recognized Whirlwind.

Believing that he had been a prisoner of the bear, they asked him if he would like to go home with them and try to rid himself of his bear nature. Whirlwind replied that he would go with them, but explained that he would have to stay alone in a house for seven days without food or water in order to become as a man again.

While the hunters were loading the meat on their backs, Whirlwind piled leaves over the place where they had killed the bear, carefully covering the drops of blood. After they had walked a short distance down the mountain, Whirlwind looked behind him. He saw a bear rise up out of the leaves, shake himself, and go back into the cave.

When the hunters reached their village, they took Whirlwind to an empty house, and obeying his wishes barred the entrance door. Although he asked them to say nothing to anyone of his hairiness and his bear nature, one of the hunters must have told of his presence in the village because the very next morning Whirlwind's wife heard that he was there.

She hurried to see the hunters and begged them to let her see her long missing husband.

"You must wait for seven days," the hunters told her. "Come back after seven days, and Whirlwind will return to you as he was when he left the village twelve moons ago."

Bitterly disappointed, the woman went away, but she returned to the hunters each day, pleading with them to let her see her husband. She begged so hard that on the fifth day they took her to the house, unfastened the door, and told Whirlwind to come outside and let his wife see him.

Although he was still hairy and walked like a bear on hind legs, Whirlwind's wife was so pleased to see him again that she insisted he come home with her. Whirlwind went with her, but a few days later he died, and the Cherokees knew that the bears had claimed him because he still had a bear's nature and could not live like a man. If they had kept him shut up in the house without food until the end of the seven days he would have become like a man again. And that is why in that village on the first warm and misty nights of springtime, the ghosts of two bears—one walking on all fours, the other walking upright—are still seen to this day.

How Antelope Carrier Saved the Thunderbirds and Became the Chief of the Winged Creatures
(Arikara)

Among the Arikaras lived a young boy whose parents were so poor that the Wood Rats took pity upon him and made for him four magic arrows. The arrows were shaped from dogwood, and the shafts were fletched with Wood Rat hide instead of feathers. One of the arrows was black, another red, another yellow and another white. After presenting the boy with the arrows, the Wood Rats made him a bow of thick hickory wood.

Whenever the boy went hunting with his magic arrows he

killed as many antelopes as his parents needed. No matter how far away an antelope might be, when the boy shot one of his arrows it always found its target. The people of his tribe marveled at his skill and named him Antelope Carrier.

After his parents grew old and died, Antelope Carrier decided to go adventuring toward the setting sun to see what the world was like. One day on his wanderings he came to a very large lake surrounded by brushes and reeds. Wild game was plentiful there, and the mountains mirrored in the lake's waters were so beautiful that he decided to stay for several days. With his bow and arrows he soon supplied himself with plenty of meat. He then built a big fire, roasted the meat, ate until he was no longer hungry, and lay down to sleep.

While he slept, two Thunderbirds glided quietly down from the sky, lifted him up and carried him to the highest of the mountains bordering the lake. When Antelope Carrier awoke, he found himself in a very strange place. The mountaintop was level but was no larger than the floor of a tepee, with steep cliffs on three sides and a dark forest descending sharply on the fourth. Antelope Carrier wondered if he would ever be able to get down from the mountaintop. On one side of the flat summit he found a nest built of sticks and soft feathers, and inside it were four young Thunderbirds.

As he sat down beside a small pool bubbling from the rock, he heard a roaring like a strong wind, and a shadow passed between him and the sun. Looking up, he saw a mother Thunderbird. She alighted close beside him and spoke to him: "My son, do not be afraid. I brought you to this place for a purpose. I have watched you for many days and know that you are a great hunter. I brought you here to help me save your young brothers in that nest. The god of the winged creatures, Nesaru, placed me and my mate upon this high place. We have been here a long time. I have built many nests and laid many eggs, but soon after my young birds hatch, a monster that lives in the big lake below always comes and destroys them. We have never raised any young Thunderbirds to take our places, and now I beg you to help me. If you can save my children I will give you what power I possess."

"What manner of monster is this that you cannot overcome it?" Antelope Carrier asked.

"It is a water serpent with two long heads, and it has a thick covering of flint stones. When I hurl my lightning upon it, the monster is not harmed. Even when I throw my lightning in its mouth, the water serpent does not die because its flint-stone covering protects every part of its body. Stay here and help me kill this monster, and you shall have lightning in your eyes, and your breath, and then you shall have control of all the birds in the whole world."

Antelope Carrier thought for a few moments. "I owe much to the wild creatures of the earth," he replied. "I will stay here and help you."

The Thunderbird thanked him and flew high in the sky to keep watch for the monster in the lake. As Antelope Carrier had not eaten since the Thunderbirds brought him to the mountain-top, he descended the east bluff into the dark forest to search for wild game. The timber was filled with birds of many colors, but he left them undisturbed and searched until he found an antelope which he killed with one arrow. He carried the meat and some sticks of wood back to the mountaintop, and made a fire with flint sparks.

While he was roasting the meat he heard the young Thunderbirds crying. He looked into their nest and saw that their mouths were wide open for food. Cutting some of the meat into small pieces, he began feeding the young birds. A moment later he heard a roaring of wings. The birds' parents swooped down and thanked him for his kindness. "We are glad you are here to help us," the father Thunderbird said. "The feathers of our young birds are beginning to turn dark, and we know it is nearly time for the monster serpent to crawl out of the lake and climb this cliff to kill and eat our children. If you see a fog rising from the lake, you will know that the serpent is coming. We will fly high into the sky now so that we can hurl our most powerful lightning down upon it."

The next morning Antelope Carrier arose early to watch the sun come up in the east. He sat down, with his bow and arrows placed in easy reach, and just as the sun was lighting the forest something made him glance toward the lake. He saw a small roll of fog rising from the middle of the waters. The fog spread as it rose higher, and after a while it covered the lake and the land around and seemed to reach into the sky.

He saw something crawling from one end of the lake, and then suddenly there was another movement some distance from the first one. Through the mists Antelope Carrier saw that they were the two heads of a serpent monster. Slowly it came crawling up the steep cliff.

About this time dark clouds rolled in from the west accompanied by rapid lightning flashes and thunder. Rain beat down upon the crawling monster and the storm swept the fog away. Soon the Thunderbirds appeared in the sky, and Antelope Carrier knew that they had brought the storm. They spread their huge wings and threw streaks of lightning down upon the serpent, but they could not stop the monster. In a few minutes one of its ugly heads reached the summit. The young Thunderbirds tumbled out of their nest in fright, and the mother bird dived with a terrifying scream. She hurled bolts of lightning into the open mouth of the monster, forcing it away from the summit, but it stubbornly began crawling back up the face of the rock.

Exhausted, the Thunderbird circled the summit, making a wailing noise. "It is all over," she cried in despair. "We cannot do any more. We have failed and must fly away. And you, my son, will have to die with my children."

Antelope Carrier watched until her weary wings lifted her above the clouds, and then he picked up his bow. From his four magic arrows he chose the black one. He fitted it to his bowstring, ready to shoot into the mouth of the monster as soon as it crawled upon the summit again. As one of the serpent's heads slithered across the flat rock, its mouth opened to swallow Antelope Carrier. He pulled his bowstring and shot deep into its red throat.

A great noise resounded across the mountain. It was like the crashing of a falling tree, and indeed the black arrow had miraculously transformed itself into a sycamore filled with many sharp branches. The monster's head burst open and dropped down the cliff. But the second head now lifted above the edge of the summit, jerking itself toward Antelope Carrier. Quickly he fitted the red arrow to his bowstring and its speeding force lifted off the second head of the monster, sending it bouncing down the bluff until it smashed into pieces upon the sharp rocks.

The Thunderbirds, who had been watching from the clouds, plunged down with cries of joy. At the same time from the dark woods thousands of birds of many colors flew up to join their musical voices in a song of triumph.

"My son," said the mother Thunderbird, "today you are chief of all the winged creatures. I give to you the power that the gods have given me. Lightning shall be in your breath and eyes. I give you a stick that shall have lightning, so that you can stun anything you strike. Wherever you go, the birds will follow you. They will warn you of monsters and other wicked animals and guard you with their power. Let us now go down where the serpent is."

They found the serpent monster broken in two, its covering of flint rock shattered into thousands of pieces. For the first time in many years the lake was smooth and without a trace of fog. When the birds saw what Antelope Carrier had accomplished they brought him berries and seeds and in this way transferred their secret magic to him.

Antelope Carrier was now chief of all the winged creatures and wherever he went the birds followed him. Whenever a monster or wicked animal appeared, the birds brought him news of it and he went and killed the beast. Although he never returned to the Arikaras, as long as he roamed over the land as chief of all winged creatures he always kept the name his people had given him—Antelope Carrier.

Why Dogs Have Long Tongues
(Caddo)

A long time ago when the animals were like people, most dogs were great talkers and liked to tell everything they knew. In those days there were not as many dogs as now, but almost every family kept a few hounds to take with them on hunts. A Caddo named Flying Hawk did not have a dog because he hated to have someone always tattling on him and telling everything he did. But he was a good hunter, and knew that he could bring back much more meat for his family if he had a trustworthy dog to help him find wild game.

One day a friend offered Flying Hawk his choice of a small puppy from a litter, and he decided to take one and try to teach it not to talk so much. He took the puppy home, and every day he spent several hours trying to teach it not to be a tattler like other dogs. The puppy soon grew big enough to be taught to hunt, and Flying Hawk began taking it out to track rabbits and other small game.

Every time that Flying Hawk killed any game, however, the dog would sneak back to the Caddo village on Red River and tell everybody about it. Then he would return to Flying Hawk in a roundabout way and come up to him from behind as though he had been there hunting all the time. Flying Hawk soon discovered that the dog was deceiving him, and he punished and scolded the animal. After each punishment the dog would stop running off and tattling for a little while, but soon he would begin again.

After a while the dog was big enough to go far away into the high timber to hunt with his master. One day Flying Hawk packed a supply of food and told the dog they were going to the Ouachita Mountains to hunt for several days. He loaded his horses with provisions and started out, with the dog his only companion. Three days of traveling brought them to the mountains and there they made camp.

"We are a long distance from our village," Flying Hawk said to his dog. "But if you go back there ahead of me and tell everything about this hunt, I will pull out your tongue."

They hunted for several days and killed many game animals. As soon as the horses were packed with all the meat they could carry, Flying Hawk and his dog broke camp and started home. During the first day's journey the dog disappeared. Flying Hawk called and searched for hours and at last decided to return to the camp-site, thinking that the dog might have lost its way and gone back there. He could not find it anywhere, however, and after another day of searching gave up the dog for lost and again started home.

Flying Hawk was so sure that he had broken the dog of sneaking home and telling everything, that he did not even consider the possibility that it might have gone on ahead of him to the Caddo village. But a few days later when he brought his laden horses home he found the dog sitting there under a tree telling tall tales about the large number of bears, mountain lions, deer and coyotes that it had tracked for Flying Hawk in the high timber.

At the sight of his prattling dog, Flying Hawk became angrier than he ever had before. "I warned you," he shouted, "that if you ran home ahead of me and told everything you know, that I would pull out your tongue!" He caught the dog and gave it a sound whipping. Being still very angry, he grabbed hold of the dog's tongue, pulled it out as far as he could, and then ran a stick across its mouth. Ever since then dogs have had long tongues and big mouths.

The Great Shell of Kintyel
(Navaho)

In the days when Kinniki, the chief of all the Eagles, lived on earth he sent the Wind spirit to persuade a certain young Navaho to leave his people and journey to Chaeo Canyon. There the Navaho was told to live as a beggar just outside the pueblo of Kintyel. Many wealthy people lived in Kintyel, and hidden somewhere in an *estufa*—one of their secret council rooms—was the largest sea shell in the world. The shell had been brought many miles across mountains and deserts from the Great Ocean where the sun goes down, and the people of Kintyel treasured it above all things.

Because these Pueblo people were always robbing Eagles' nests and making prisoners of the young birds, the chief of the Eagles decided to punish them by taking their great shell from them. But first the hiding-place of the shell had to be found, and that is why the young Navaho was sent there—to pose as a miserable beggar while he kept a lookout for the location of the shell.

Taking the name Nahoditahe, the Navaho dressed in rags and prowled around Kintyel, pretending to search in kitchen heaps and room sweepings for bits of bread and corn grains. One afternoon as he was leaving his crude shelter outside the pueblo, he noticed two young men gesturing excitedly toward Standing Rock Mountain. They had sighted a War-Eagle soaring in the sky. Nahoditahe watched the Eagle move slowly away, growing smaller and smaller against the blue until it descended upon one of the crags of Standing Rock. Nahoditahe also saw the two young men cut a forked stick and drive it into the ground fork upward, placing it so that when they stood in a certain position and sighted over it they could find the exact spot where the Eagle had landed. They left the stick standing and hurried away toward Kintyel.

Eagles were very scarce in the Pueblo country because the people had captured or killed so many for their feathers, and the news that one had been sighted caused much excitement. The next morning Nahoditahe saw four chiefs from the Kintyel clans come out from the town to take sightings over the forked stick. After a while they started off toward Standing Rock. About nightfall they returned with news that they had found an Eagle's nest with two fine young eaglets inside it.

The only way to reach the nest, however, was to lower a man to it with a rope. Because the rope would have to pass over a protruding ledge, the task would be difficult and dangerous. The chiefs asked for volunteers, but no one appeared willing to risk the endeavor even for such rich prizes as young Eagles. While they were debating the matter in a council room, someone suggested they try the Navaho beggar.

A messenger was sent for Nahoditahe and when he came to the council room they gave him bowls of boiled corn and meat, a basket of wafer bread, and other choice foods. Nahoditahe had not seen so many good things to eat since he left the Navaho country, and he ate as he had never eaten before. When he had finished, he thanked the Pueblos for their generosity.

"If you will do what we ask of you," they said, "you shall eat of such abundance all your life and never again have to scrape for grains of corn among the dirt and ashes." They told him of their plan for capturing the young Eagles and asked him if he were willing to be lowered to the nest in a basket held by ropes.

Nahoditahe saw at once that this would give him an opportunity to help his friends the Eagles, but he pretended to be fearful of such an undertaking. He sat silent for a long time as though pondering the risks, and then after each of the chiefs begged him to accept, he answered them. "I lead but a poor life at best," he said. "Existence is not sweet to a man who is always hungry. It would be pleasant to eat such food as you have given me for the rest of my days. I shall do as you wish."

During the night the Pueblos' best basket-makers wove a strong carrying-basket with four corner loops at the top. Next morning they gave the Navaho a good breakfast, and then he and the chiefs —with a large party accompanying them—set out for Standing Rock. They carried the basket, some strong rope, and a large piece of netting.

When they reached a ledge below the Eagles' nest, the men carrying the netting turned off, the others climbing on to the top. There they fastened the rope to the four corners of the basket and told Nahoditahe to get inside. "When we lower you to the nest," they said, "take the eaglets out and drop them into the netting that the men are holding down below."

Nahoditahe stepped into the basket and the Pueblos lowered him slowly over the edge of the precipice. After a minute or so the basket stopped. "Lower me farther," the Navaho called up to them. Again the basket dropped until it was level with the nest. "Stop!" he shouted. His voice and sudden appearance frightened the young Eagles.

He felt a cool breath of air, and then the Wind spirit was all around him, whispering: "These people, the Pueblos, are not your friends. They do not intend to keep their promise of providing you with good food as long as you live. If you drop these young Eagles into the net, they will never pull you up again. Get into the Eagles' nest and stay there."

The Navaho then called to the Pueblos above: "Swing the basket nearer the cliff. I can't reach the nest unless you do so." The men swung the rope until the basket rocked against the cliff, and Nahoditahe scrambled quickly into the big nest, leaving the empty basket swaying in the air.

Although the Pueblos could see the empty basket swinging, they waited, expecting to see the Navaho climb back into it. But after waiting a long time, they began calling to him. "My son," cried the old men, "throw down the little Eagles." And the young men shouted: "Brother, throw down the little Eagles!" They kept up their pleading until nearly sunset, but the Navaho never replied. He sat quietly in the rock crevice, and when the sun went down the Pueblos stopped calling to him and went home.

Early the next morning they returned and gathered in a large crowd at the foot of the cliff. All day long they begged him to drop the eaglets to them, making many promises, and showing him all kinds of tempting food. But the Navaho remained silent. For two more days, they came to the base of the cliff, their anger rising against Nahoditahe. They shouted curses at him and then shot fire-arrows into the rock crevice in hopes of setting fire to the nest and compelling him to throw it and the eaglets down. But he was watchful, and whenever a fire-arrow landed he seized it quickly and flung it out.

On the fourth day, the Navaho spoke to the young birds: "Can you not help me?" The eaglets replied by rising from their nest and shaking their wings, throwing out many tiny feathers. When these feathers floated down upon the people below, they left in fear that the Eagles were putting a curse upon them. As they went away they shouted to Nahoditahe that they were leaving him there to die.

After his tormentors were gone, the Navaho wondered how much longer he could endure hunger and thirst. As darkness fell, a wave of despair swept over him, and then he heard a great rushing sound, a roaring of giant wings. Two Eagles, a male and a female, landed on the nest. "Thank you, brother," the male Eagle said. "For your bravery we name you Kinniki after the chief of all the Eagles in the sky."

"I am hungry," the Navaho replied. "I am thirsty."

The Eagle opened the sash around his waist and drew out a small bag of cornmeal, a bowl made from a white shell, and a horsetail plant. The joints of the horsetail plant, which grows near streams, were filled with water, and the Eagle mixed some of the water with the cornmeal and handed the bowl to the Navaho. After the man had eaten, he drank his fill from the jointed horsetail plant.

As it was now dark, with a chill wind blowing across the mountains, the Eagles invited him to sleep between them in the nest. For the first time since he had come to Standing Rock, Nahoditahe slept warm, and he did not waken until he heard voices calling from the top of the cliff: "Where are you? The day has dawned. It is growing late. Why are you not abroad already?" At the sound of the voices, the Eagles also awoke, and the Navaho soon discovered that the callers were Eagles and Hawks. Presently dozens of them began circling in front of the crevice, and then an Eagle landed beside the nest.

"I have brought our brother a dress of plumes so that he can escape from here," he said, and started to put the feathers around the Navaho. But the male Eagle in the nest raised a wing in objection. "This would not be well," he said. "Our brother is heavy and has not yet learned to fly." The two argued for a few minutes, other Eagles and Hawks coming to join in the discussion, and then they all flew up to the summit to hold council.

When they returned, they told the Navaho they had thought of a better plan to rescue him from the rock crevice. "Lie flat on your belly," the male Eagle said. After Nahoditahe stretched himself out on the rock, a pair of Eagles flew down with a streak of crooked lightning and placed it under his feet. Other Eagles brought a sunbeam and put it under his knees, and a rainbow to support his forehead. Then three streaks of straight lightning were placed beneath his body.

An Eagle then seized each end of these supports—twelve Eagles in all—and they flew with the Navaho and the eaglets away from the crevice. They circled twice with their burden before rising above Standing Rock, and then circled twice more, climbing toward the south. When they passed above Mount Taylor they circled four more times until they almost touched the sky. Now they were beginning to tire, and Nahoditahe heard them cry out: "We are weary. We can fly no farther." But soon they sighted the sky-hole, and with renewed effort lifted their wings to fly him through the entrance and into the Upper World above the sky.

Safely landed, Nahoditahe found himself surrounded by four pueblos—a white town on the east, a blue town on the south, a yellow town on the west, a black town on the north. He went with the Eagles into the white town, and as soon as they were inside their houses they took off their feather suits, hung them up on pegs, and went around in white suits which they wore under their plumage. They served him wafer bread and other good food.

That evening a number of War-Eagles returned, and they were received with loud wailing and tears. The Navaho soon learned that a large war party had gone out that morning, but many had not returned. They had been slain in battle.

In all the excitement of war, the great shell of Kintyel was forgotten. Nahoditahe found no one interested in discussing it with him. During the next few days the Eagles spent all their time organizing another war party, and the morning they started out on the trail, the Navaho decided to accompany them.

"Where are you going?" they asked him.

"I wish to join your war party," he replied.

They laughed at him and said: "You are a fool to think you can go to war against such dreadful enemies as those we fight. We can move as fast as the wind, yet our enemies can move faster. If they are able to overcome us, what chance have you, a poor man, for your life?"

They went on, traveling on foot, the Navaho following at a distance. When they camped for the night, he joined them, and this time they spoke to him angrily, ordering him to return to the pueblos at next daylight.

In the morning, when the War-Eagles resumed their march, Nahoditahe remained behind on the camping ground as though he intended to return, but as soon as they were out of sight he followed them. He had not traveled far when he saw a plume of smoke rising from the ground, and as he came nearer he found a smoke-hole in which stood a ladder, yellowed from the smoke. He looked down and saw in the room below a strange-looking old woman with a big mouth. Her curved teeth protruded from her mouth, and he knew that she was Spider Woman—she who had taught the Navahos how to weave. She invited him to come down the ladder.

As soon as he was inside her house she showed him her four magic hoops—one black, one blue, one yellow, one white. Attached to the hoops were several ragged feathers. "These feathers," she said, "were once beautiful plumes but now they are old and dirty. I must have new plumes for my hoops, and you can get them for me. Many of the Eagles will be killed in the battle to which you are going, and when they die you must pluck out their feathers and bring them to me."

Nahoditahe drew back from her. "Ah," she said, "you need have no fear of their enemies." She laughed. "Do you know who they are that the Eagles go to fight? They are only bumblebees and tumbleweeds." She gave him a long black cane and a stalk of yellow-flowered snakeweed. "With this cane you can conquer the tumbleweeds. When the bumblebees come, chew the snakeweed and spit its juice upon them and they cannot sting you. But before you destroy the tumbleweeds, take some of their seeds, and after you have killed the bees take some of their nests filled with their young. You will need these things when you return to the earth. Go now to the field of battle."

The Navaho traveled on until he saw the Eagles hiding behind a little hill. They were preparing for battle by painting themselves and putting on their plumes. From time to time one of them would creep cautiously up to the top of the hill and peer over. Then he would run back and report: "The enemies are gathering. They await us." Curious to see the enemies, Nahoditahe crept to the hilltop and peered over. He could see no enemies, nothing but a dry sandy flat covered on one side by a mass of sunflowers, and on the other by dead weeds.

About this time the Eagles raised their war cry and charged over the hill into the sandy plain. Watching from the hilltop, the Navaho saw a whirlwind arise. A great number of tumbleweeds surged upward in a swirl of dust and spun madly through the air. At the same time from among the sunflowers a swarm of bumblebees arose.

The Eagles charged through the ranks of their enemies, and when they had passed to the other side they turned around and charged back again. Some spread their wings and soared aloft to attack the tumbleweeds that had gone up with the whirlwind. From time to time the dark body of an Eagle fell crashing to earth. After the combat had continued for some time, a few of the Eagles came running toward the hill where Nahoditahe lay watching. In a moment, others began fleeing the field, and soon the whole war party, all that was left of it, rushed past him in disorderly retreat, leaving many Eagles slain on the ground. Then the whirlwind played itself out, the tumbleweeds lay quiet again on the ground, and the bumblebees disappeared among the sunflowers.

As soon as all was quiet, the Navaho walked down the hill slope and gathered up some tumbleweed seeds, tying them into a corner of his shirt. With his black cane he pushed all the tumbleweeds into a pile and set them on fire. He took out the snakeweed that Spider Woman had given him and chewed on it until his mouth was filled with juice. Then he walked among the yellow sunflowers.

All at once the bumblebees swarmed around him, trying to sting him, but he spat the snakeweed juice upon them. Those he struck fell stunned to the ground and the others fled in fear. He killed all that he could find and then dug some of their nests out of the ground. Capturing two of the young bees, he tied their feet together and put them in a corner of his blanket. And then, remembering the wishes of Spider Woman, he went around among the dead Eagles, plucking as many plumes as he could carry.

Setting out upon his return journey, he soon reached the house of Spider Woman and gave her the plumes. "Thank you, my grandchild," she said. "You have brought me the feathers that I needed, and at the same time you have done a great service for your friends, the Eagles, because you have slain their enemies."

That night he had to camp on the trail, but the following morning he reached the pueblos of the Eagles. As he approached the houses he could hear the Eagles crying in their grief for fallen comrades. They crowded around him. "We have lost many of our kinsmen," they said, "and we are wailing for them. We have also been mourning for you, because those who returned told us you had been killed in the battle."

Nahoditahe made no reply, but he took the two young bumblebees from his blanket and swung them around his head. At sight of the bees, the Eagles were terrified and ran, and they did not stop running until they had concealed themselves behind their houses. Soon they overcame their fears, and crowded around the Navaho again. Once more he showed them the bees, and again they ran away in terror. A third and a fourth time, Nahoditahe played with the bees to prove to the Eagles that they no longer had reason to fear them. Then he placed the two bees on the ground and took out the tumbleweed seeds and laid them beside the bees. "My friends," he said, "here are the children of your enemies. Look upon them and know that I have slain your enemies."

There was great rejoicing among the Eagles when they heard this, and the chief of the white pueblo led Nahoditahe into his house and showed him the finest room that the Navaho had ever seen. Its smooth walls were coated with white earth, and its furnishings were of the highest quality. Logs burned brightly in a fireplace which was surrounded by mealing-stones, beautiful pots, and water jars. "My son," said the chief, "this house is yours."

Throughout the day the chiefs and leaders from all the pueblos came to thank Nahoditahe for the great service he had done for them. They brought him eight large bowls, each containing food of a different kind. They brought him beautiful feather robes and blankets and spread them on the floor for his bed.

Next morning he went over to the sky-hole, taking with him the young bees and the tumbleweed seeds. To the bees he said: "Go down to the land of the Navahos and multiply there. In the days to come my people will make use of you and your honey, but if you ever cause them sorrow and trouble as you have caused the Eagles I shall again destroy you." As he spoke, he flung them down to the earth. Then taking the tumbleweed seeds in his hands, he spoke to them as he had spoken to the bees, and threw them down through the sky-hole.

For twenty-four more days, Nahoditahe remained in the Upper World with the Eagles. During this time they taught him their songs, prayers, and sacrifices, which he was to take back to his people for their bead chant ceremony. When he had learned all the rites, the Eagles told him it was time for him to return to earth and continue his search for the great shell of Kintyel.

They dressed him in one of their robes of eagle plumes and escorted him to the sky-hole. "When we brought you from the Lower World you were heavy and had to be carried," they said. "Henceforth you shall float in the air as we do and move with your own power." He spread his wings and the Eagles blew a powerful breath behind him. Down he went through the sky-hole, gliding past the clouds until he landed gently on the summit of Mount Taylor.

The Wind spirit was waiting for him there. "The rich people of Kintyel are suffering from a strange sickness," the Wind spirit said. "They are searching for a powerful medicine-man who can cure their sickness. They will give their richest treasures for such a cure, anything except their great shell. Do not be fooled if they bring you a shell that you can embrace and still touch your fingertips together. The great shell is larger than that."

When Nahoditahe reached Kintyel and walked among the houses, no one recognized him. Well-fed, handsome, and splendidly clothed, he bore no resemblance to the poor beggar these people had left to die in the Eagles' nest on Standing Rock. He noticed that there were many lame people in the pueblo, and when he asked the reason for this he was told that a strange sickness had broken out among them.

"I have been taught the secrets of a powerful medicine-man," Nahoditahe said. "I believe I know a ceremony that will cure this sickness."

The chiefs invited him to meet with them in council, and Nahoditahe told them that he could drive the sickness away with a night chant. "I will lead the dancers," he said, "but I must be dressed in a particular way. I must have strings of fine beads—shell and turquoise—enough to cover my legs and forearms completely, and enough to go around my neck so that I cannot bend my head back. Lastly I must have the largest shell in Kintyel to hang on my back. Four days from now I will be ready to perform the night chant and drive the sickness away."

On the next day the chiefs brought him beads of shell and turquoise, the finest they could collect among all the people, and on the second day they brought him several large shell basins from which to choose to wear upon his back. He measured the shells with his arms as the Wind spirit had told him to do, but his hands joined easily. "None of these is large enough," he said, and they brought him larger and larger shells. Each time they tried to persuade him that the shells were the largest they had, but Nahoditahe rejected all.

On the last day, with much reluctance, they brought him the great shell of Kintyel, and when he clasped it in his arms his fingers did not meet on the opposite side. "This," he said, "is the shell I must wear when I dance."

That evening Nahoditahe ordered them to build a great circle of pine branches, such as the Navahos now build for the rites of their mountain chant. As darkness fell, a great crowd gathered in the enclosure, and fires were lighted around the circle.

Nahoditahe now put on his robe of plumes, covered his arms and legs and neck with the rich beads of the Pueblos, and fastened the great shell of Kintyel upon his back. He led the dancers out into the circle and began to dance. As he danced, he chanted a song about the rising up of white, blue, yellow, and black corn.

This seemed a strange song to the Pueblo people, and they all wondered what it could mean. They soon found out what it meant. To their great astonishment the dancing Navaho began rising slowly from the ground. First his head and then his shoulders rose above the heads of the crowd. Soon his chest and waist lifted above them, but not until his whole body had risen above the level of their heads did they begin to realize the loss that threatened them.

Nahoditahe was rising toward the sky with the great shell of Kintyel and all the wealth of many Pueblos in shell-beads and turquoise. They screamed wildly to him to come down again, but the more they shouted the higher he rose. A dark cloud had formed above him in the starlit sky, and from it lightning streaked beneath his feet. The gods were lifting him to the Upper World. In desperation the people of Kintyel threw ropes up to seize and pull him back to earth, but he was beyond reach of their longest rope. The chiefs shouted for arrows to shoot him down, but before one could be fixed to a bow the Navaho was lost to sight in the black cloud.

Not since that day has the great shell of Kintyel been seen upon this earth. The old men say that it is in one of the pueblos of the Upper World, closely guarded by the War-Eagles of Kinniki.

The Girl Who Climbed to the Sky
(Arapaho-Caddo)

One morning several young women went out from their tepee village to gather firewood. Among them was Sapana, the most beautiful girl in the village, and it was she who first saw the porcupine sitting at the foot of a tall cottonwood tree. She called to the others: "Help me to catch this porcupine, and I will divide its quills among you."

The porcupine started climbing the cottonwood, but the tree's limbs were close to the ground and Sapana easily followed. "Hurry," she cried. "It is climbing up. We must have its quills to embroider our moccasins." She tried to strike the porcupine with a stick, but the animal climbed just out of her reach.

"I want those quills," Sapana said. "If necessary I will follow this porcupine to the top of the tree." But every time that the girl climbed up, the porcupine kept ahead of her.

"Sapana, you are too high up," one of her friends called from the ground. "You should come back down."

But the girl kept climbing, and it seemed to her that the tree kept extending itself toward the sky. When she neared the top of the cottonwood, she saw something above her, solid like a wall, but shining. It was the sky. Suddenly she found herself in the midst of a camp circle. The treetop had vanished, and the porcupine had transformed himself into an ugly old man.

Sapana did not like the looks of the porcupine-man, but he spoke kindly to her and led her to a tepee where his father and mother lived. "I have watched you from afar," he told her. "You are not only beautiful but industrious. We must work very hard here, and I want you to become my wife."

The porcupine-man put her to work that very day, scraping and stretching buffalo hides and making robes. When evening came, the girl went outside the tepee and sat by herself wondering how she was ever to get back home. Everything in the sky world was brown and gray, and she missed the green trees and green grass of earth.

Each day the porcupine-man went out to hunt, bringing back buffalo hides for Sapana to work on, and in the morning while he was away it was her duty to go and dig for wild turnips. "When you dig for roots," the porcupine-man warned her, "take care not to dig too deep."

One morning she found an unusually large turnip. With great difficulty she managed to pry it loose with her digging stick, and when she pulled it up she was surprised to find that it left a hole through which she could look down upon the green earth. Far below she saw rivers, mountains, circles of tepees, and people walking about.

Sapana knew now why the porcupine-man had warned her not to dig too deep. As she did not want him to know that she had found the hole in the sky, she carefully replaced the turnip. On the way back to the tepee she thought of a plan to get down to the earth again. Almost every day the porcupine-man brought buffalo hides for her to scrape and soften and make into robes. In making the robes there were always strips of sinew left over, and she kept these strips concealed beneath her bed.

At last Sapana believed that she had enough sinew strips to make a lariat long enough to reach the earth. One morning after the porcupine-man went out to hunt, she tied all the strips together and returned to the place where she had found the large turnip. She lifted it out and dug the hole wider so that her body would go through. She laid her digging stick across the opening and tied one end of the sinew rope to the middle of it. Then she tied the other end of the rope about herself under her arms. Slowly she began lowering herself by uncoiling the lariat. A long time passed before she was far enough down to be able to see the tops of the trees clearly, and then she came to the end of the lariat. She had not made it long enough to reach the ground. She did not know what to do.

She hung there for a long time, swinging back and forth above the trees. Faintly in the distance she could hear dogs barking and voices calling in her tepee village, but the people were too far away to see her. After a while she heard sounds from above. The lariat began to shake violently. A stone hurtled down from the sky, barely missing her, and then she heard the porcupine-man threatening to kill her if she did not climb back up the lariat. Another stone whizzed by her ear.

About this time Buzzard began circling around below her. "Come and help me," she called to Buzzard. The bird glided under her feet several times, and Sapana told him all that had happened to her. "Get on my back," Buzzard said, "and I will take you down to earth."

She stepped on to the bird's back. "Are you ready?" Buzzard asked.

"Yes," she replied.

"Let go of the lariat," Buzzard ordered. He began descending, but the girl was too heavy for him, and he began gliding earthward too fast. He saw Hawk flying below him. "Hawk," he called, "help me take this girl back to her people."

Hawk flew with Sapana on his back until she could see the

tepee of her family clearly below. But then Hawk began to tire, and Buzzard had to take the girl on his back again. Buzzard flew on, dropping quickly through the trees and landing just outside the girl's village. Before she could thank him, Buzzard flew back into the sky.

Sapana rested for a while and then began walking very slowly to her parents' tepee. She was weak and exhausted. On the way she saw a girl coming toward her. "Sapana!" the girl cried. "We thought you were dead." The girl helped her walk on to the tepee. At first her mother did not believe that this was her own daughter returned from the sky. Then she threw her arms about her and wept.

The news of Sapana's return spread quickly through the village, and everyone came to welcome her home. She told them her story, especially of the kindness shown her by Buzzard and Hawk.

After that, whenever the people of her tribe went on a big hunt they always left one buffalo for Buzzard and Hawk to eat.

II
Before the White Men Came

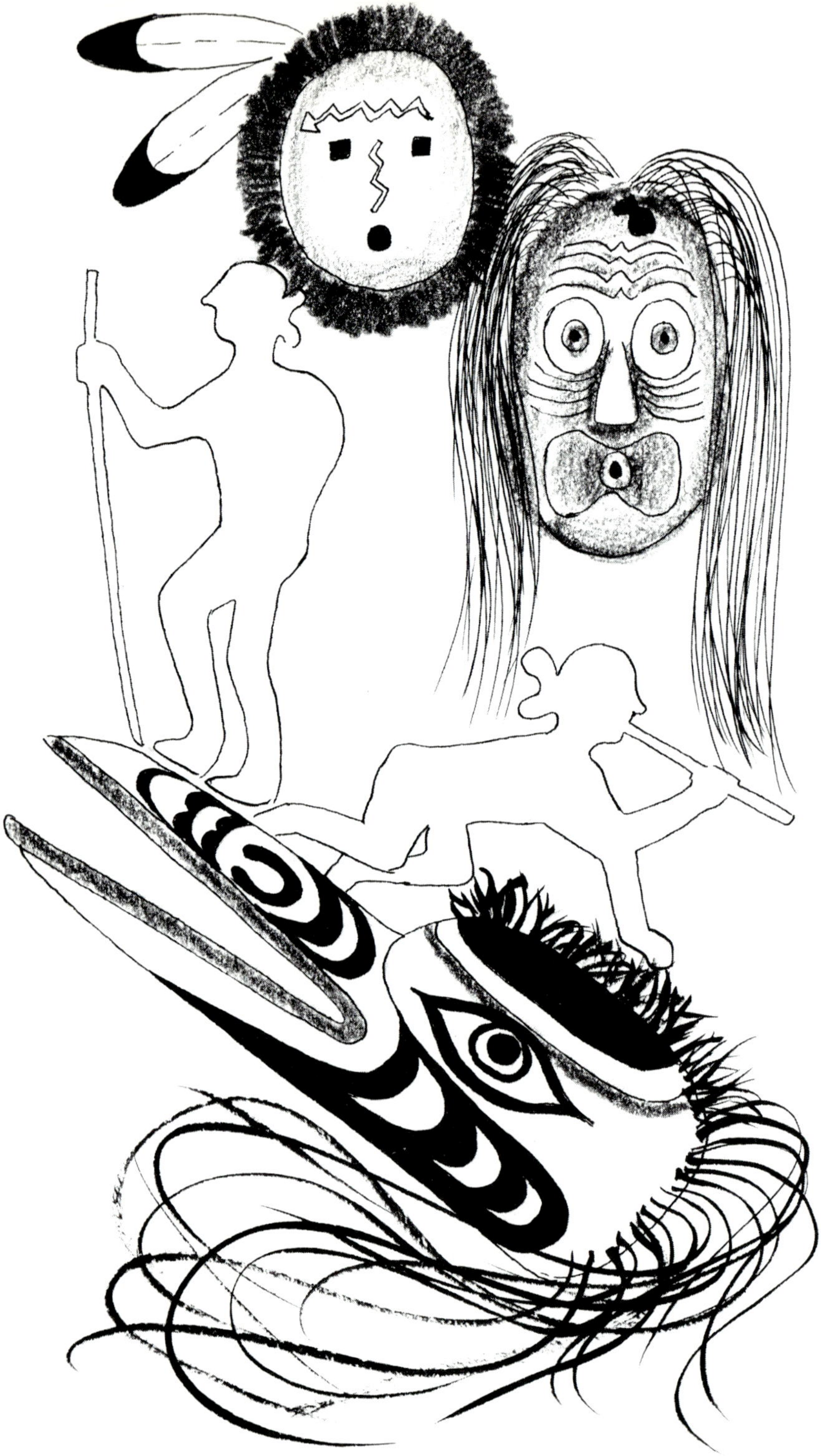

Long before Europeans came to America, storytellers of almost every tribe created legends about various culture heroes, many of them probably being based upon real persons. These heroes are as old or older than Beowulf, and like Beowulf they performed wondrous deeds. They saved their people from disasters and often established the social and political organizations of their tribes.

One of the best preserved hero legends is that of Motzeyouf or Sweet Medicine, several versions of which exist. It was Sweet Medicine who brought the four sacred arrows to the Cheyennes and founded the tribe's warrior societies, including the famous Dog Soldiers. Like several other culture heroes, he was also a prophet who warned of the coming of light-skinned bearded men from the East.

Closely related to the hero legends were the origin myths. For the Blackfeet, Old Man was the creator of all things, but other tribes have numerous legends of the origins of the most important elements of Indian life such as the buffalo, corn, fire, and their spoken languages.

The Cheyenne Prophet
(Cheyenne)

Long ago when the Cheyenne people first roamed the Western Plains, an orphan boy named Motzeyouf lived in a tepee with his grandmother. In those days the Cheyennes were poor. A buffalo-calfskin robe and a pair of moccasins were all the clothing that Motzeyouf owned. Because he burned sweetgrass in his grandmother's lodge and perfumed his robe with the smoke, some of his friends began calling him Sweet Grass. Later on, after he learned to work magic, they sometimes called him Sweet Medicine.

As Motzeyouf grew older, his grandmother noticed that he often disappeared from the tepee at night. When he returned from these mysterious ventures, he would astonish the people in his camp with remarkable feats. He could make buffalo appear and disappear, and performed many other deeds of magic. To give himself these powers he wore his buffalo robe with the hair turned outside and always carried a down feather of an eagle.

Young Wolf, the chief of the Cheyennes, became jealous of Motzeyouf because the boy was admired by all who knew him. The Cheyennes had not chosen Young Wolf to be their chief, but instead they feared him because he and his warriors ruled by force, taking what they wanted from the people. In those days, the Cheyennes had no tribal organization, and there seemed to be no way they could rid themselves of Young Wolf's injustices.

At certain times the old medicine men of the tribe would gather in one of the larger tepees to seek some way to destroy the tyranny of Young Wolf. Although these men possessed extraordinary powers, none of them was wise enough in magic to perform superhuman deeds. When Motzeyouf reached the age of seventeen, the medicine men decided to hold an incantation dance, and they invited the boy to attend. They were curious to see how strong his magic might be in the performance of a medicine dance.

Motzeyouf did not seem surprised to receive the invitation. In preparation for the medicine dance he painted his body red, with black stripes around his face and each wrist and ankle. He then placed a bowstring made from a buffalo sinew around his neck and a yellow eagle feather in his hair. Wearing only his ragged buffalo-calfskin robe and carrying a bundle of sweetgrass, he strode confidently into the lodge of the medicine men.

The old men made him welcome, and asked him where he wished to sit in their circle. He chose the right-hand side of the lodge. After they had feasted on buffalo meat and smoked from the ceremonial pipe, one of the medicine men began the performances. While dancing, each man in turn performed some remarkable feat. They passed arrows through their bodies, ejected large stones from their mouths, and swallowed coals of fire.

Soon it was Motzeyouf's turn. He started his dance very slowly, then gradually increased the tempo. He tightened the noose of the bowstring around his neck, passing the ends to two of the medicine men, motioning them to pull harder and harder. Suddenly he dropped to his knees, flung his bundle of sweetgrass into the lodge fire, and when the fragrant smoke arose he covered his head with his robe. To the astonishment of the medicine men, Motzeyouf's head then appeared to roll from his body, his neck severed by the tightened bowstring. Motzeyouf's body fell forward toward the severed head, and an instant later he leaped from the smoke, his body whole once again.

With their moccasined feet, the medicine men pounded the tepee floor. They grunted loud approvals: "Huh-huh-huh!" Their eyes brightened with admiration. "The boy has great power," said one of the old men. "Truly, Motzeyouf is one of the greatest medicine dancers of the Cheyennes."

Early the next morning the Cheyennes broke camp and started moving westward. Buffalo were scarce in the valley in which they had been living, and scouts moved out ahead of the column in search of a new herd. In that time the Cheyennes had no horses, and dogs were used to drag the camp equipment on travois—sledges made from two tepee poles and a piece of tepee cover. Everybody except the smallest children walked. Motzeyouf joined a group of teenage boys scouting along a ridge, and on the morning of the second day of the march they sighted a small buffalo herd grazing along a dry creek just below.

Slipping quietly down the ridge, they were able to get within bowshot of several calves. Motzeyouf claimed a black yearling, and brought it down with one swift arrow. "At last," he cried, "I shall have a new robe." The remaining calves escaped to join the herd which was galloping away.

Although none of the other boys had been as lucky as Motzeyouf, they rushed forward to help him skin his calf with their bone knives.

"Skin it very carefully," Motzeyouf cautioned them. "I want a robe without a hole in it."

While they were working, Young Wolf, the man who called himself chief of the Cheyennes, came up behind them. Young Wolf had heard the old medicine men praise Motzeyouf for his magical powers, and the chief's jealousy of the boy had grown into active dislike. "What a fine buffalo calf," Young Wolf said. "This is just the sort of buffalo I have been looking for."

By this time the boys had removed the glossy black hide, and Motzeyouf began rolling it up. "You are welcome to all the meat," he told the chief politely, "but I wish to keep the skin. As you can see, the robe I wear is in tatters."

"No," replied Young Wolf angrily, "I want the skin also." He tried to pull it away from the boy, and the hide fell upon the ground. When Young Wolf bent to pick it up, Motzeyouf took one of the buffalo legs which had been cut off and struck the chief on the back of the head with the hard hoof. Young Wolf fell face down without uttering a sound.

"You've killed him!" one of the boys shouted. "Young Wolf's warriors will kill you now." They all ran away in fear, leaving Motzeyouf alone.

Motzeyouf did not know what to do. With his buffalo hide slung over his shoulder, he walked along the sandy bed of the dry creek, keeping concealed in the willows until darkness fell. Then he climbed to the top of the ridge. He could see the campfires of the Cheyennes in the distance. He approached very carefully so as not to alarm the dogs and set them to barking. At last he found his grandmother's tepee and hurried inside.

"I struck Young Wolf and killed him," he told her.

The old woman shook her head. "Young Wolf is not dead. The blow only stunned him. He came here very angry, looking for you."

Although Motzeyouf was relieved to learn that he had not slain the chief, he knew that Young Wolf and his warriors would not rest until they had punished him severely. They would surely beat him with clubs until he was crippled or dead.

His grandmother wept for him as she stirred a big pot of soup. "No one blames you for what you did," she said. "The boys who were with you told everyone that Young Wolf tried to seize your buffalo calfskin."

"He and his warriors will return, looking for me." The boy took several sticks of dry wood and placed them on the red coals around the earthen soup pot. The fire crackled, sparks flying up to the smoke-hole of the tepee. "Grandmother," he said, "when they come for me again, tip the pot of soup into the fire."

As Motzeyouf foresaw, the chief and his warriors soon returned. He could hear them outside the tepee, surrounding it, and calling his name. After a moment they pushed their way inside, and Motzeyouf's grandmother tipped the pot of soup into the fire. The hot embers exploded and a cloud of steam filled the tepee. Afterwards some of the warriors said that Motzeyouf simply vanished in the smoke. Others said that he changed himself into an eagle feather and floated out through the smoke-hole. In their anger they tore down the tepee searching for him.

All through the night Motzeyouf was running, running until his breath burned his lungs. He climbed the high ridge, crossed the ravine, and ran until he fell exhausted in a thicket of brush and trees. As he lay on the leaf-covered ground he prayed to the Great Medicine to tell him what to do.

During the days that followed around the temporary camps of the Cheyennes, several mysterious events occurred. Not until long afterward did the people understand the meaning of these strange happenings. One morning Motzeyouf showed himself plainly on the edge of the camp. Atop his head was the skin of a buffalo bull's head, with the horns left on. Strapped around his waist was a belt of buffalo hide, with the animal's tail hanging down. Fastened to one of his heels was the beard of a buffalo bull. His face and body were painted bright red, and an eagle feather was in his hair. As soon as Young Wolf's warriors sighted Motzeyouf, they rushed in pursuit, believing they had trapped him in a horseshoe-shaped coulée, or ravine. They found nothing but a buffalo bull which galloped away with a stream of arrows flying harmlessly after it.

Next day the watchful warriors saw Motzeyouf roasting meat over a little fire at the foot of the ridge. When they tried to capture him, the boy concealed himself in a thicket of wild plums. The warriors rushed into the brush, beating the ground with their clubs, but only a coyote ran out to disappear down the creek. The baffled warriors returned to the cooking fire where a piece of meat was still smoking. Leading up to the fire were the moccasin prints of Motzeyouf, but going away from it they found nothing but coyote tracks.

Then, for a few days, there was no sign of Motzeyouf. The Cheyennes moved their camp a few miles farther toward the setting sun, and again Motzeyouf showed himself, this time with black paint over his body. He was carrying an elk-hoof rattle and a crook-ended lance. When the warriors went in pursuit, they saw only an elk running far away along a ridge.

The next time he appeared—wearing the skin and feathers of an owl across his forehead and carrying a stringless bow in one hand—the warriors were waiting for him. This time Young Wolf ordered the entire camp to surround the trees in which Motzeyouf took cover. They beat the underbrush and examined every tree, but when they came to the last tree only an owl flew out, making a mocking cry.

Several days passed with no sign of Motzeyouf, and then one morning Young Wolf saw smoke rising out of some willows along the nearby creek. Summoning his warriors, the chief hurried with them down the slope. Only a few yards ahead of them, Motzeyouf suddenly appeared in a little clearing. He was wearing a long shoulder-belt of rawhide decorated with bright-colored porcupine quills and rows of eagle feathers. When the warriors sprang after him, the boy vanished in the willows. A few moments later they found one of the camp dogs there, its tongue hanging out, panting as though from hard running.

All these magic things Motzeyouf performed because the Great Medicine had come to him in a vision, instructing him how to do them. He was not seen again by the Cheyennes for many, many moons. Not until he returned did they understand that in his mysterious appearances Motzeyouf was showing them the future societies of the tribe—the Red Shield warriors, the Coyotes, the Elks, the Bow Strings, and the Cheyenne Dog Soldiers. It was these societies that later would make the Cheyennes one of the strongest of all the tribes on the Western Plains.

After his last appearance, Motzeyouf started toward the rising sun, walking and running until he came to *Paha Sapa*, the Black Hills. There he found a holy mountain, the one that today the people call Bear Butte. On one side of the mountain he found a thick flat rock that was like a door, and when he came close to it, the mountain opened for him and he found himself inside an immense tepee. Four old men welcomed him in. "Grandson," said one of them, "we have been waiting for you."

Around a council fire in the enormous lodge sat dozens of young men. Some were red-skinned, some black-skinned, and some white-skinned with hair on their faces. They had come from nations all over the earth to learn from the Great Medicine. At the back of the lodge the Great Medicine, whose hair was long and white, was standing to welcome Motzeyouf. The Great Medicine pointed to a stone seat, the only empty place around the council fire. Beside the seat was a magic bundle wrapped in foxskin, and Motzeyouf saw similar bundles resting at the feet of all the other young men.

"If you take that seat," said the Great Medicine, "you must stay with us for many moons so that we may teach you to become the prophet of your people, the Cheyennes."

Motzeyouf did not hesitate. He took the empty seat, and in the days that followed the spiritual men began teaching him the things he must know to become a prophet. The Great Medicine—who had made the sun, the moon, the stars and the earth—taught him supernatural powers. He learned sacred songs and dances. He learned how to see far into the future. He was given the secret of the four societies and the council of forty-four chiefs that he was to take back to the Cheyennes so the tribe could protect itself from the rule of a single cruel chief.

Only one test did Motzeyouf fail. When he was asked which of the young men around the council fire he would choose to be like, he thought for a long time. The handsomest and the strongest was a light-skinned man with hair on his face, and Motzeyouf at last pointed to him. The Great Medicine shook his head. "You have made a bad choice," he said. "The light-skinned man will turn everything to stone, and then he will turn himself to stone."

During the last moon that Motzeyouf stayed in the sacred mountain he was told to open the magic foxskin bundle which lay beside his place at the council fire. Inside were four arrows, each as long as a man's leg. The flintstone points were covered with white down feathers of an eagle, and fixed to the shaft ends were whole wing feathers of an eagle. The feathers and shafts were dyed with blue and brown paint to represent the colors of the sky and the earth. Along two of the arrows were pictures of buffalo and other animals. Along the others were figures of men and tepees.

"These four arrows possess magic," the Great Medicine said. "Two have power over animals, two have power over human beings. If enemies threaten your people, turn the points of the man-arrows toward them and they will become confused and crazy and run away. When a buffalo herd is sighted, turn the points of the buffalo-arrows toward them and they will run in a circle so the hunters can walk among them and kill as many as may be needed. The four arrows symbolize the power that you will bring to your people. They must be kept in a sacred tepee, and the magic they hold must be renewed by ceremonies of songs and dances that we will teach you."

As soon as Motzeyouf learned the ceremonies of renewal, the spiritual men painted his body red and told him to return to his people. "They will welcome you as a prophet," the Great Medicine said. "While you have been here, the Cheyennes have been wandering without purpose. The wild game shun them, and they are weak and hungry. Young Wolf and many of his warriors were killed when they tried to take meat from another tribe. Go find your people and show them how to live."

For many days Motzeyouf searched for the Cheyennes, and at last far up in the hills he found their poor camp. As he approached he saw four children digging in the earth for roots. Their clothing was ragged, their rib bones pressed against their skin, and their faces were pinched from hunger.

"Is this all you can find to eat?" he asked quietly. "Roots and moss?"

The children stopped their digging and looked up at him. Although Motzeyouf was taller and his hair much longer than when they had last seen him, some of the children remembered him. "You are Motzeyouf, Sweet Medicine, who was driven away by the warriors many moons ago," said one.

"I have come back, only to find my people starving."

"The buffalo are all gone," the boy replied. "We cannot find even rabbits or mice to eat. Nothing but roots and mushrooms and moss. In the moons of strong cold we almost died."

Motzeyouf kneeled to face the children. "Find for me some old buffalo bones. Bring me buffalo bones and you shall have meat to eat."

They looked at him strangely, and then went off to search. When they returned with the bones, Motzeyouf spread his robe on the ground and told them to place the bones upon it. He folded the robe over the bones so that the corners pointed to the four directions, and when he opened it again the bones had changed to pemmican and marrow fat. "Eat," Motzeyouf said.

The astounded children ate until they were no longer hungry and there was still much meat left. "Take this food into camp," Motzeyouf said, "and tell your parents that Motzeyouf the Prophet has returned. Tell them I can bring back the buffalo so they will no longer be hungry and cold."

As soon as the children were out of sight, Motzeyouf hurried after them, circling the camp until he found a tepee which bore the markings of his grandmother. She was sitting outside in the sun, her eyes closed, her face wrinkled with age. He slipped inside and found a pallet of old buffalo skins that she still kept for him. He lay down and pulled his robe over his head.

After a few minutes he heard voices outside. The people of the tribe were gathering, asking for him. His grandmother told them she had not seen Motzeyouf, but she came into the tepee and found a tall young man lying on her grandson's pallet. He was dressed in red leggings and moccasins and wore an eagle down feather in his hair. "My grandson!" she cried. "You have come back!"

Hearing her outcry, the people pushed into the lodge to welcome Motzeyouf the Prophet. The medicine men remembered the magical powers of his boyhood, and when he told them that he had been with the Great Medicine in the Black Hills, they knew that he was now a man of strong visions. "Take pity on us," an old man begged him. "The people are mourning and crying for food. Tell us what we must do that the Cheyennes can live again."

Motzeyouf showed them his bundle of magic arrows. "I have brought you four powerful and holy arrows," he said. "They will make us a great people. Go and place all your tepees in a circle, with their openings to the rising sun. In the middle of the circle, erect the largest tepee of all. Bring your pipes and rattles there, and I will teach you the songs and ceremonies of the sacred arrows that have been taught to me. We will bring back the buffalo."

By the time everything was ready, the sun was setting. The medicine men gathered wood and built a big fire in the center of the double-sized tepee. Just as darkness fell, Motzeyouf brought an old buffalo skull and a bundle of sweetgrass. He placed the buffalo skull in the entrance of the lodge and scattered sweetgrass over the fire so that the air was filled with fragrance.

Then he began singing one of the songs he had learned in the Black Hills, and as he sang he removed one of the sacred arrows from the foxskin bundle and began the first ceremony. As the song came to an end, the men in the lodge could hear the hooves of buffalo rumbling in the distance.

"They are the leaders coming ahead of the herds," Motzeyouf said, and he began singing the second song over the second arrow. "These arrows," he declared, "will bring us a new life." When the second song ended, the hoofbeats of the buffalo were louder. Herds were approaching from the four directions.

During the singing of the third song, they could hear buffalo grunting and puffing. "Wait," Motzeyouf warned the impatient medicine men. "Stay within the lodge." He began the fourth song, and as he sang the sound of the great herds outside the camp was like the roaring of thunder. At last Motzeyouf finished the fourth ceremony of the arrows. "Go now and sleep," he said. "The buffalo will no longer shun the Cheyenne people. They will give us our food, shelter, and clothing. When the sun rises go and kill only what you need."

"Will the buffalo stay with us forever, Sweet Medicine?" asked one of the old men.

Motzeyouf stared into the flames of the lodge fire. After a long time he replied: "The buffalo will not leave us until bearded strangers come into our country."

Next morning the land in all directions was covered with buffalo, and the hunters went out with bows and arrows to kill what they needed. For the first time in many moons the Cheyennes feasted, all afternoon and into the night, on the choicest meats— on buffalo tongue and buffalo hump and marrow fat.

To make the tribe strong, Motzeyouf now began to teach his people how they must protect themselves from a bad leader such as Young Wolf had been. There was much to learn, he warned them. Instead of one chief they would have forty chiefs, with four additional warrior chiefs.

And so the people gathered and chose their chiefs, and then Motzeyouf explained the mysterious appearances he had made before leaving for the holy mountain in the Black Hills. These represented warrior societies that would hold the Cheyennes together against all ordeals, against all enemies. Many moons passed while the men formed four warrior societies—the Coyotes or Swift Foxes, the Elks or Hoof-Rattles, the Bowstrings, and the Red Shields.

During this time there was much controversy over the dress, the symbols, the songs and dances of the different societies, and especially over which young men would be members. At last after everything was settled Motzeyouf noted that several young men had not been chosen for any of the societies. This was because they were poor or were unlucky at hunting, or had demonstrated no powers of magic. Motzeyouf went to one of them, a young man named Little Hawk, and told him to go through the camp announcing that he wanted followers for a new society.

"But I am a nobody," Little Hawk replied. "No one will listen to me."

"Do as I tell you," Motzeyouf promised. "They will follow you."

As the young man went through the camp crying for followers, the warrior society members laughed at him. No one came to join him and at sunset Little Hawk sat in the middle of the camp circle and began chanting a sacred song that Motzeyouf had taught him. While he sang, the camp dogs began whining and howling.

When midnight came, Little Hawk walked out through the opening of the camp circle and all the dogs in camp followed him. Even the puppies came, the females carrying in their mouths those too young to walk. Little Hawk led them down to a level place along a river bottom, and when he came to a tree that leaned toward the north he sat down to rest his back against the trunk. To his surprise, the dogs formed themselves into a half circle, facing him. In a dream, some mysterious power caused a tepee to spring up around him and the tree, and the dogs rushed toward the entrance. As soon as they entered the tepee they turned into human beings. On their left sides they wore shoulder-belts of animal skins decorated with bright-colored feathers and porcupine quills. Their headdresses were caps, with beads decorating the fronts and with erect feathers of eagles, crows and hawks covering the sides and crowns. They carried wingbone whistles ornamented with porcupine quills and wore rattles shaped like snakes. Their belts were skunk skins, with the animals' heads left intact.

Until sunrise they danced and sang to Little Hawk, promising him that the Dog Soldiers would be the most powerful of all the Cheyenne societies. And then he fell into a deep sleep.

In the morning the Cheyennes awakening in camp were amazed to discover that all their dogs were missing. Two men went searching, and down on the grassy flats they found a mysterious tepee around a tree that leaned toward the north. In front of it, the dogs of the tribe sat in a semi-circle facing the entrance. Hurrying back to camp, the two Cheyennes sought out Motzeyouf and told him of what they had seen.

"A young man waits for us in that tepee," Motzeyouf said. "He is obeying the commands of the Great Medicine who is using our dogs to show us how to form the strongest warrior society, the Cheyenne Dog Soldiers."

News of this strange happening spread quickly through the camp, and on the advice of the medicine men the Cheyennes moved their tepees down to the river and placed them in a circle around Little Hawk's magic lodge. The dogs rejoined their owners, many of whom then went to ask Little Hawk to choose them as members of his society. From that day, the Dog Soldiers flourished as the bravest of the Cheyenne societies, and until the coming of light-skinned strangers from the East, no tribe was more prosperous or more powerful than the Cheyennes.

Through the years they listened well to Motzeyouf the Prophet, who guided them through his visions. He lived to be very old, one of the oldest men who ever lived among the Cheyennes, and then one autumn day while the tribe was camped near the place we call Devil's Tower (in Wyoming), he summoned the people together to say goodbye to them for the last time.

"My brothers, my children, I have lived on earth as long as the Great Medicine wishes me to live. My body is bent and crooked, but I have seen beyond many moons far into the future. Listen! Listen to me and remember my words. They are sharp as the points of the four holy arrows. The Great Medicine put us on earth. He made us, but he also made others. Some are red as we are, some are black, some are light-skinned with hair on the faces of their men. One day soon you will meet the light-skinned hairy people by the Great Muddy River. They will be clad in strange clothing and will carry sicknesses of all kinds.

"They will offer you strange presents—a white sand that melts in the mouth and tastes sweet—things that flash in the sunlight and reflect your faces as water in a quiet stream does when you look into it. They will give you something to drink, something that is like water but contains an invisible fire. If you drink, it will make you crazy like the men who give it to you. Do not take the things they offer you. You will begin to act foolishly and forget all the people who lived before you. If you take these things, they will bring a sickness upon you.

"These light-skinned strangers will speak no Indian tongue. They will be restless and cruel, never tiring, always going, going toward the setting sun. They will hunt for yellow stones in the earth, and will kill each other for these stones. They will kill all the buffalo and the other wild game. They will not kill a few animals with arrows or spears, but more than they can use with long sticks that make loud noises and smoke, and send round pieces of metal through the air so fast that eyes cannot see them.

"From the south they will bring a strange animal with flashing eyes, long hair on its neck, and a tail that reaches to the ground. Its hoofs will be round, not split like a buffalo's. Fear not this animal. It will carry you on its back and take you to places farther than the rim of the earth. They will bring another strange animal, spotted, with long horns, big eyes, and a long tail. They will eat this animal as we do the buffalo, and after they have killed all the buffalo they will try to make you eat the tough stringy meat of the spotted animal.

"They will come to us on the rivers, floating upon strange objects that go up and down blowing smoke. They will not listen to what you say to them, but will make you listen to what they say to you. If you listen to them, you will start quarreling among yourselves as in the old days before the warrior societies and the forty-four chiefs.

"My brothers, my children, keep your own ways, do not follow the ways of the strangers. Even if you are strong against them, they will ask for your children to teach them their way of living, to rub out all our past deeds, our beliefs, our way of speaking. Our children will then know nothing, and the strangers will take everything from us. They will kill all the animals, destroy all the trees, and foul the waters of the streams. They will rip the earth apart and make you do it with them. And then they and you and the earth will turn to stone forever.

"Remember the holy arrows. Renew them. Keep my prophecies in your hearts, and the Cheyennes will endure as long as the blue heavens endure."

This was Motzeyouf's farewell to his people. He asked the leaders of the warrior societies to build a shelter for him some distance from the camp. They built it of cedar poles covered with grass and bark, and then heaped sweetgrass on the earthen floor for him to lie upon. "Leave me," he told them. They went away, and in the next moon when they returned they could find no sign of Motzeyouf. He was never seen again.

The Deeds and Prophecies of Old Man
(Blackfoot)

Old Man came from the south, traveling north. As he moved along he made the mountains, plains, timber and brush, putting rivers here and there, fixing up the world as we see it today. Old Man covered the plains with grass for the animals to feed upon. He marked off certain pieces of ground, and made all kinds of roots and berries grow in the earth—wild carrots, wild turnips, serviceberries, bull berries, cherries, plums and rosebuds. He put trees in the ground.

After Old Man made the Porcupine Hills, he took some mud and shaped it into human forms. He blew breath upon them and they became people. He made men and women, and named them Siksika, or Blackfeet. They asked him: "What are we to eat?" He replied by making more images of clay in the forms of buffalo. Then he blew breath on these and they stood up, and when he made signs to them, they started to run. "These are your food," Old Man said to the Siksika.

After he had made the buffalo, Old Man went out on the plains and made the bighorn, a sheep with a big head and horns. Because it was awkward and could not move fast, the bighorn did not travel easily on the level prairies. And so Old Man took it by one of its horns and led it up into the mountains and turned it loose. There it skipped about among the rocks and went up high places with ease. "This is the place that suits you," Old Man said. "This is what you are fitted for, the rocks and the mountains."

While he was in the mountains, Old Man made the antelope and turned it loose, but the antelope ran so fast that it fell over some steep rocks and hurt itself. He saw that this would not do, so he carried the antelope down on to the plains where he turned it loose. It ran away swiftly and gracefully, and Old Man said: "This is what you are suited for."

One day Old Man decided to make a woman and a child. He went to a river-bank, took some wet clay, and molded it into human shapes. Then he covered them up with straw. The next morning he took the covering off and told the images to rise and walk, and they did so, following him down to the river. "I am Napi," he told them. "Old Man, the maker of all things."

As they were standing by the river, the woman said to him: "How is it? Will we always live? Will there be no end to it?"

"I have never thought of that," Old Man replied. "We will have to decide it." He picked up a buffalo chip and threw it in the river. "If the buffalo chip floats," he said, "when people die, they will come back to life again after four days. But if it sinks, when they die that will be an end to them." When he threw the chip in the river, it floated.

The woman did not like the thought of dying, even for only four days. "No, we should not decide it that way," she said. She picked up a stone. "If the stone floats, we will always live," she said. "If it sinks, people will die forever." She threw the stone into the river and it sank to the bottom.

"There," said the woman. "Perhaps it is better for people to die forever. Otherwise they would never feel sorry for each other and there would be no sympathy in the world."

"Well," said Old Man. "You have chosen. Let it be that way. Let that be the law."

Not long afterwards, the woman's child died, and she went to Old Man, pleading with him to change the law about people dying. "You first said that people who die will come back after four days," she said. "Let that be the law."

"Not so," Old Man replied. "What is made law must be law. We will undo nothing that we have done. The child is dead, and it cannot be changed. People will have to die."

About this time many of the Siksika people that Old Man had made came to him with complaints that they did not know how to hunt the buffalo and obtain meat. Instead, the buffalo were hunting them, they said, running after them and killing some people.

"I will make you a weapon that will kill these animals," Old Man promised. He went out and cut some serviceberry shoots and brought them in and peeled the bark off them. He then caught a bird and took some feathers from its wing. After tying these feathers to one of the serviceberry shoots, he broke a black flintstone into pieces and fastened a sharp flint point to one of the shoot ends and named it an arrow. Then he took a large piece of wood, shaped it, strung it, and named it a bow.

While the people watched, he showed them how to use bows and arrows. "Next time you hunt buffalo," he said, "take these things with you and use them as I have instructed you. Do not run from the buffalo. When they run at you, wait until they are close enough and shoot them with arrows."

After the people had learned to kill buffalo, Old Man showed them how to take the skins from them to make robes. He showed them how to set up poles and fasten the skins on them to make tepees to sleep under.

One day Old Man told the Siksika that it was time for him to move on north to make more land and more people. "I have marked off this land for you," he said. "The Porcupine Hills, Cypress Mountains, and Little Rocky Mountains, down to the mouth of the Yellowstone on the Missouri, and then toward the setting sun to the head of the Yellowstone and the tops of the Rocky Mountains. There is your land, and it is full of all kinds of animals, and many things grow in this land. Let no other people come into this land, or trouble will come to you. This land is for the five tribes, the Blackfeet, Bloods, Piegans, Gros Ventres and Sarcees. If other people try to cross the line, take your bows and arrows and give them battle and keep them out. If you let them come and make camp, you will lose everything."

For many moons the five tribes gave battle to all other people who tried to cross the line made by Old Man, and kept them out. But after a while some bearded men with light skins came, bringing presents. They said they wanted to stay only a little while to trap animals for their furs. The five tribes let them make camp, and as Old Man had prophesied, the tribes soon lost everything.

How Day and Night Were Divided
(Creek)

After the world was made, some of the animals wanted the day to last all the time. Others preferred that it be night all the time. They quarreled about this and could come to no agreement. After a while they decided to hold a meeting, and they asked Nokosi the Bear to preside.

Nokosi proposed that they vote to have night all the time, but Chew-thlock-chew the Ground Squirrel said: "I see that Wotko the Raccoon has rings on his tail divided equally, first a dark color then a light color. I think day and night ought to be divided like the rings on Wotko's tail."

The animals were surprised at the wisdom of Chew-thlock-chew. They voted for his plan and divided day and night like the dark and light rings on Wotko the Raccoon's tail, succeeding each other in regular order.

But Nokosi the Bear was so angry at Chew-thlock-chew for rejecting his advice that he thrust out a paw and scratched the

Squirrel's back with his sharp claws. This is what caused the thirteen stripes on the backs of all his descendants, the Ground Squirrels.

How the Buffalo Were Released on Earth
(Apache-Comanche)

In the first days a powerful being named Humpback owned all the buffalo. He kept them in a corral in the mountains north of San Juan, where he lived with his young son. Not one buffalo would Humpback release for the people on earth, nor would he share any meat with those who lived near him.

Coyote decided that something should be done to release the buffalo from Humpback's corral. He called the people to a council. "Humpback will not give us any buffalo," Coyote said. "Let us all go over to his corral and make a plan to release them."

They camped in the mountains near Humpback's place, and after dark they made a careful inspection of his buffalo enclosure. The stone walls were too high to climb, and the only entrance was through the back door of Humpback's house.

After four days Coyote summoned the people to another council, and asked them to offer suggestions for releasing the buffalo. "There is no way," said one man. "To release the buffalo we must go into Humpback's house, and he is too powerful a being for us to do that."

"I have a plan," Coyote said. "For four days we have secretly watched Humpback and his young son go about their daily activities. Have you not observed that the boy does not own a pet of any kind?"

The people did not understand what this had to do with releasing the buffalo, but they knew that Coyote was a great schemer and they waited for him to explain. "I shall change myself into a killdeer," Coyote said. "In the morning when Humpback's son goes down to the spring to get water, he will find a killdeer with a broken wing. He will want this bird for a pet and

63

will take it back into the house. Once I am in the house I can fly into the corral, and the cries of a killdeer will frighten the buffalo into a stampede. They will come charging out through Humpback's house and be released upon the earth."

The people thought this was a good plan, and the next morning when Humpback's son came down the path to the spring he found a killdeer with a crippled wing. As Coyote had foreseen, the boy picked up the bird and carried it into the house.

"Look here," the boy cried. "This is a very good bird!"

"It is good for nothing!" Humpback shouted. "All the birds and animals and people are rascals and schemers." Above his fierce nose Humpback wore a blue mask, and through its slits his eyes glittered. His basket headdress was shaped like a cloud and was painted black with a zig-zag streak of yellow to represent lightning. Buffalo horns protruded from the sides.

"It is a very good bird," the boy repeated.

"Take it back where you found it!" roared Humpback, and his frightened son did as he was told.

As soon as the killdeer was released it returned to where the people were camped and changed back to Coyote. "I have failed," he said, "but that makes no difference. I will try again in the morning. Perhaps a small animal will be better than a bird."

The next morning when Humpback's son went to the spring, he found a small dog there, lapping at the water. The boy picked up the dog at once and hurried back into the house. "Look here!" he cried. "What a nice pet I have."

"How foolish you are, boy!" Humpback growled. "A dog is good for nothing. I'll kill it with my club."

The boy held tight to the dog, and started to run away crying.

"Oh, very well," Humpback said. "But first let me test that animal to make certain it is a dog. All animals in the world are schemers." He took a coal of fire from the hearth and brought it closer and closer to the dog's eyes until it gave three rapid barks. "It is a real dog," Humpback declared. "You may keep it in the buffalo corral, but not in the house."

This of course was exactly what Coyote wanted. As soon as darkness fell and Humpback and his son went to sleep, Coyote opened the back door of the house. Then he ran among the buffalo, barking as loud as he could. The buffalo were badly frightened because they had never before heard a dog bark. When Coyote ran nipping at their heels, they stampeded toward Humpback's house and entered the rear door. The pounding of their hooves awakened Humpback, and although he jumped out of bed and tried to stop them, the buffalo smashed down his front door and escaped.

After the last of the shaggy animals had galloped away, Humpback's son could not find his small dog. "Where is my pet?" he cried. "Where is my little dog?"

"That was no dog," Humpback said sadly. "That was Coyote the Trickster. He has turned loose all our buffalo."

Thus it was that the buffalo were released to scatter over all the earth.

How Corn Came to the Earth
(Arikara)

A long time ago giants lived on the earth, and they were so strong they were not afraid of anything. When they stopped giving smoke to the gods of the four directions, Nesaru looked down upon them and was angry. "I made the giants too strong," Nesaru said. "I will not keep them. They think that they are like me. I shall destroy them by covering the earth with water, but I will save the ordinary people."

Nesaru sent the animals to lead the ordinary people into a cave so large that all the animals and people could live there together. Then he sealed up the cave and flooded the earth so that all the giants drowned. To remind himself that people were under the ground waiting to be released after the floodwaters were gone, Nesaru planted corn in the sky. As soon as the corn ripened, he took an ear from the field and turned it into a woman. She was the Mother-Corn.

"You must go down to the earth," Nesaru told her, "and bring my people out from under the ground. Lead them to the place where the sun sets, for their home shall be in the west."

Mother-Corn went down to the earth, and when she heard thunder in the east she followed the sound into the cave where the people were waiting. But the entrance closed behind her, and she could find no way to lead the people out upon the earth. "We must leave this place, this darkness," she told them. "There is light above the ground. Who will help me take my people out of the earth?"

The Badger came forward and said: "Mother-Corn, I will help." The Mole also stood up and said: "I will help the Badger dig through the ground, that we may see the light." Then the long-nosed Mouse came and said: "I will help the other two."

The Badger began to dig upwards. After a while he fell back exhausted. "Mother-Corn, I am very tired," he said. Then the Mole dug until he could dig no more. The long-nosed Mouse took the Mole's place, and when he became tired, the Badger began to dig again. The three took turns until at last the long-nosed Mouse thrust his nose through the ground and could see a little light.

The Mouse went back and said: "Mother-Corn, I ran my nose through the earth until I saw light, but the digging has made my nose small and pointed. After this all the people will know by my nose that it was I who dug through the earth first."

The Mole now went up to the hole and dug all the way through. The sun had come up from the east, and it was so bright it blinded the Mole. He ran back and said: "Mother-Corn, I have been blinded by the brightness of that sun. I cannot live upon the earth any more. I must make my home under the earth. From this time all the Moles will be blind so they cannot see in the daylight, but they can see in the night. They shall stay under the ground in the daytime."

The Badger then went up and made the hole larger so the people could go through. When he crawled outside the Badger closed his eyes, but the rays of the sun struck him and blackened his legs and made a streak of black upon his face. He went back down and said: "Mother-Corn, I have received these black marks upon me, and I wish that I might remain this way so that people will remember that I was one of those who helped to get your people out."

"Very well," said Mother-Corn, "let it be as you say."

She then led the way out, and the people rejoiced that they were now upon the open land. While they were standing there in the sunshine, Mother-Corn said: "My people, we will now journey westward toward the place where the sun sets. Before we start, any who wish to remain here—such as the Badger, Mouse, or Mole—may do so." Some of the animals decided to return to their burrows in the earth; others wanted to go with Mother-Corn.

The journey was now begun. As they traveled, they could see a mountainous country rising up in front of them. They came to a deep canyon. The bluff was too steep for the people to get down, and if they should get down, the opposite side was too steep for them to climb. Mother-Corn asked for help, and a bluish-gray bird flew up, hovering on rapidly beating wings. It had a large bill, a bushy crest and a banded breast. The bird was the Kingfisher. "Mother-Corn," it said, "I will be the one to point out the way for you."

The Kingfisher flew to the other side of the canyon, and with its beak pecked repeatedly into the bank until the earth fell into the chasm. Then the bird flew back and pecked at the other bank until enough earth fell down to form a bridge. The people cried out their thanks. "Those who wish to join me," said the Kingfisher, "may remain here and we will make our homes in these cliffs." Some stayed, but most journeyed on.

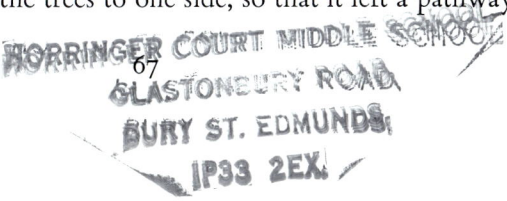

After a while they came to another obstacle—a dark forest. The trees were so tall they seemed to reach the sun. They grew close together and were covered with thorns so that they formed an impenetrable thicket. Again Mother-Corn asked for help. This time an Owl came and stood before her, and said: "I will make a pathway for your people through this forest. Any who wish to remain with me may do so, and we shall live in this forest forever." The Owl then flew up through the timber. As it waved its wings it moved the trees to one side, so that it left a pathway for the people to go through. Mother-Corn then led the people through the forest and they passed onward.

As they journeyed through the country, all at once they came to a big lake. The water was too deep and too wide to cross, and the people talked of turning back. But they could not do this, for Nesaru had ordered Mother-Corn to lead them always toward the west. A water bird with a black head and a checkered back came and stood in front of Mother-Corn, and said: "I am the Loon. I will make a pathway through this water. Let the people stop crying. I shall help them."

Mother-Corn looked at the Loon and said: "Make a pathway for us, and some of the people will remain with you here." The Loon flew and jumped into the lake, moving so swiftly that it parted the waters, and when it came out on the other side of the lake it left a pathway behind. Mother-Corn led the people across to dry land, and some turned back and became Loons. The others journeyed on.

At last they came to a level place beside a river, and Mother-Corn told them to build a village there. "Now you shall have my corn to plant," she said, "so that you, by eating of it, will grow and also multiply." After they built a village and planted the corn, Mother-Corn returned to the Upper World.

The people, however, had no rules or laws to go by, no chiefs or medicine men to advise them, and soon they were spending all their time at playing games. The first game they played was shinny ball, in which they divided into sides and used curved sticks to knock a ball through the other's goal. Then they played at throwing lances through rings placed upon the ground. As time went on, the players who lost games grew so angry that they began killing those who had beaten them.

Nesaru was displeased by the behavior of the people, and he and Mother-Corn came down to earth. He told them that they must have a chief and some medicine men to show them how to live. While Nesaru taught the people how to choose a chief through tests of bravery and wisdom, Mother-Corn taught them songs and ceremonies. After they had chosen a chief, Nesaru gave the man his own name, and then he taught the medicine men secrets of magic. He showed them how to make pipes for offering smoke to the gods of the four directions.

When all this was done, Nesaru went away toward the setting sun to prepare a place for new villages. Mother-Corn led the people in his tracks across plains and streams to this country where Nesaru had planted roots and herbs for the medicine men. There they built villages along a river that the white men later called the Republican River, in Kansas.

On the first day that they came to this country, Mother-Corn told them to offer smoke to the gods in the heavens and to all animal gods. While they were doing this, a Dog came running into the camp crying, and he accused Mother-Corn of doing wrong by going away and leaving him behind. "I came from the Sun," he cried, "and the Sun-god is so angry because I was left behind that he is sending the Whirlwind to scatter the people."

Mother-Corn called on the Dog to save the people by appeasing the Whirlwind. "Only by giving up my freedom," the Dog replied, "can I do this. No longer can I hunt alone like my brother the Wolf, or roam free like the Coyote. I shall always be dependent upon the people."

But when the Whirlwind came spinning and roaring across the land, the Dog stood between it and the people. "I shall always remain with the people," he shouted to the Whirlwind. "I shall be a guardian for all their belongings."

After the wind died away, Mother-Corn said: "The gods are jealous. If you forget to give smoke to them they will grow angry and send storms."

In the rich earth beside the river the people planted her corn, and then she said: "I shall turn into a Cedar-Tree to remind you that I am Mother-Corn, who gave you your life. It was I, Mother Corn, who brought you from the east. I must become a Cedar-Tree to be with you. On the right side of the tree will be placed a stone to remind you of Nesaru, who brought order and wisdom to the people."

Next morning a Cedar-Tree, full-grown, stood in front of the lodges of the people. Beside it was a large stone. The people knew that Mother-Corn and Nesaru would watch over them through all time, and would keep them together and give them long life.

How Rabbit Brought Fire to the People
(Creek)

In the beginning there was no fire and the earth was cold. Then the Thunderbirds sent their lightning to a sycamore tree on an island where the Weasels lived. The Weasels were the only ones who had fire and they would not give any of it away.

The people knew that there was fire on the island because they could see smoke coming from the sycamore, but the water was too deep for anyone to cross. When winter came the people suffered so much from the cold that they called a council to find some way of obtaining fire from the Weasels. They invited all the animals who could swim.

"How shall we obtain fire?" the people asked.

Most of the animals were afraid of the Weasels because they were bloodthirsty and ate mice and moles and fish and birds. Rabbit was the only one who was brave enough to try to steal fire from them. "I can run and swim faster than the Weasels," he said. "I am also a good dancer. Every night the Weasels build a big fire and dance around it. Tonight I will swim across and join in the dancing. I will run away with some fire."

He considered the matter for a while and then decided how he would do it. Before the sun set he rubbed his head with pine tar so as to make his hair stand up. Then, as darkness was falling, he swam across to the island.

The Weasels received Rabbit gladly because they had heard of his fame as a dancer. Soon they had a big fire blazing and all began dancing around it. As the Weasels danced, they approached nearer and nearer the fire in the center of the circle. They would bow to the fire and then dance backwards away from it.

When Rabbit entered the dancing circle, the Weasels shouted to him: "Lead us, Rabbit!" He danced ahead of them, coming closer and closer to the fire. He bowed to the fire, bringing his head lower and lower as if he were going to take hold of it. While the Weasels were dancing faster and faster, trying to keep up with him, Rabbit suddenly bowed very low so that the pine tar in his hair caught fire in a flash of flame.

He ran off with his head ablaze, and the angry Weasels pursued him, crying, "Catch him! Catch him! He has stolen our sacred fire! Catch him, and throw him down!"

But Rabbit outran them and plunged into the water, leaving the Weasels on the shore. He swam across the water with the flames still blazing from his hair.

The Weasels now called on the Thunderbirds to make it rain so as to extinguish the fire stolen by Rabbit. For three days rain poured down upon the earth, and the Weasels were sure that no fire was left burning except in their sycamore tree.

Rabbit, however, had built a fire in a hollow tree, and when the rain stopped and the sun shone, he came out and gave fire to all the people. After that whenever it rained, they kept fires in their shelters, and that is how Rabbit brought fire to the people.

Godasiyo the Woman Chief
(Seneca)

At the beginning of time when America was new, a woman chief named Godasiyo ruled over an Indian village beside a large river in the East. In those days all the tribes spoke one language and lived in harmony and peace. Because Godasiyo was a wise and progressive chief, many people came from faraway places to live in her village, and they had no difficulty understanding one another.

At last the village grew so large that half the people lived on the north side of the river, and half on the south side. They spent much time canoeing back and forth to visit, attend dances, and exchange gifts of venison, hides, furs, and dried fruits and berries. The tribal council house was on the south side, which made it necessary for those who lived on the north bank to make frequent canoe trips to consult with their chief. Some complained about this, and to make it easier for everybody to cross the rapid stream, Godasiyo ordered a bridge to be built of saplings and tree limbs carefully fastened together. This bridge brought the tribe close together again, and the people praised Godasiyo for her wisdom.

Not long after this, a white dog appeared in the village, and Godasiyo claimed it for her own. Everywhere the chief went the dog followed her, and the people on the north side of the river became jealous of the animal. They spread stories that the dog was possessed by an evil spirit that would bring harm to the tribe. One day a delegation from the north bank crossed the bridge to the council house and demanded that Godasiyo kill the white dog. When she refused to do so, the delegates returned to their side of the river, and that night they destroyed the bridge.

From that time the people on the north bank and those on the south bank began to distrust each other. The tribe divided into two factions, one renouncing Godasiyo as their chief, the other supporting her. Bad feelings between them grew so deep that Godasiyo foresaw that the next step would surely lead to fighting and war. Hoping to avoid bloodshed, she called all members of the tribe who supported her to a meeting in the council house.

"Our people," she said, "are divided by more than a river. No longer is there goodwill and contentment among us. Not wishing to see brother fight against brother, I propose that those who recognize me as their chief follow me westward up the great river to build a new village."

Almost everyone who attended the council meeting agreed to follow Godasiyo westward. In preparation for the migration, they built many canoes of birch bark. Two young men who had been friendly rivals in canoe races volunteered to construct a special watercraft for their chief. With strong poles they fastened two large canoes together and then built a platform which extended over the canoes and the space between them. Upon this platform was a seat for Godasiyo and places to store her clothing, extra leggings, belts, robes, moccasins, mantles, caps, awls, needles and adornments.

At last everything was ready. Godasiyo took her seat on the platform with the white dog beside her, and the two young men who had built the craft began paddling the double canoes beneath. Behind them the chief's followers and defenders launched their own canoes which contained all their belongings. This flotilla of canoes covered the shining waters as far as anyone could see up and down the river.

After they had paddled a long distance, they came to a fork in the river. Godasiyo ordered the two young canoeists to stop in the middle of the river until the others caught up with them. In a few minutes the flotilla was divided, half of the canoes on her left, the others on her right.

The chief and the people on each side of her began to discuss the advantages and disadvantages of the two forks in the river. Some wanted to go one way, some preferred the other way. The arguments grew heated with anger. Godasiyo said that she would take whichever fork her people chose, but they could agree on neither. Finally those on the right turned the prows of their canoes up the right channel, while those on the left began paddling up the left channel. And so the tribe began to separate.

When this movement started, the two young men paddling the two canoes carrying Godasiyo's float disagreed as to which fork they should take, and they fell into a violent quarrel. The canoeist on the right thrust his paddle into the water and started toward the right, and at the same time the one on the left swung his canoe toward the left. Suddenly Godasiyo's platform slipped off its supports and collapsed into the river, carrying her with it.

Hearing the loud splash, the people on both sides turned their canoes around and tried to rescue their beloved chief. But she and the white dog, the platform, and all her belongings had sunk to the bottom, and they could see nothing but fish swimming in the clear waters.

Dismayed by this tragic happening, the people of the two divisions began to try to talk to each other, but even though they shouted words back and forth, those on the right could not understand the people on the left, and those on the left could not understand the people on the right. When Godasiyo drowned in the great river her people's language had become changed. This was how it was that the Indians were divided into many tribes spreading across America, each of them speaking a different language.

III
Allegories

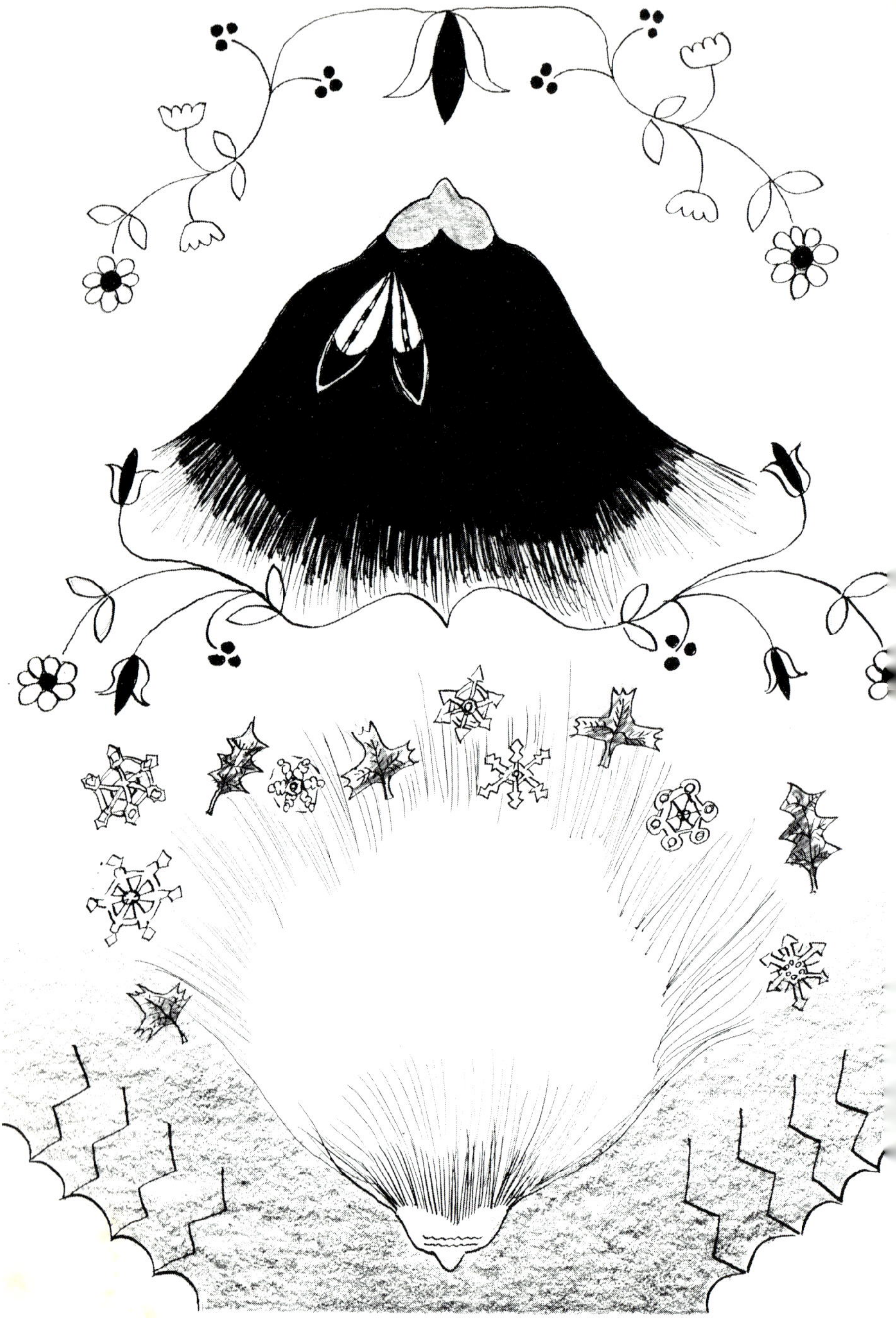

The allegory, a tale in which ideas or the forces of nature are presented as persons, is one of the oldest forms of storytelling. American Indians used short allegories to tell of the changing of the seasons, and they were very popular among the Eastern tribes of North America. This Cherokee story of the power of winter and a Chippewa tale of the coming of springtime are representative of Indian symbolic tales.

The Return of Ice Man
(Cherokee)

Once during the autumn in the Great Smoky Mountains some dry leaves in the woods caught fire, and before the people could beat out the flames the fire spread to a big poplar tree. The tree blazed fiercely until it turned to ashes, and then the fire went down into the roots and burned a great hole in the ground. It burned and burned, and the hole grew constantly larger, until the people became frightened and were afraid it would burn the whole world. Time after time they tried to extinguish the fire, but it had gone too deep, and they did not know what to do.

At last a chief said that Ice Man was the only one who could put out the fire, and he lived in a house of ice far away to the north. The chief called the people together for a council to choose two messengers to journey northward in search of Ice Man.

After traveling a long distance the messengers found Ice Man. He was a very old person with long hair hanging down to the ground in two plaits. The messengers told him why they had come to ask his help.

"Oh, yes," replied Ice Man, "I can help you put out that fire." He began to unplait his long hair. When it was all unbraided, he took a thatch of it in one hand and struck it across his other hand, and the messengers felt a chill wind blow against their faces. A second time he struck his hair across his hand, and a light rain began to fall. The third time he struck his hair across his open hand, sleet rattled upon the ground, and when he struck the fourth time a heavy snow began to fall, as if it had come from the ends of his hair.

"Go back to your village," Ice Man said, "and I shall be there in a few days." The messengers speedily returned to their people, who were still gathered helplessly around the great burning pit.

A few days later, while they were all fearfully watching the fire, a strong wind blew from the north, and they knew it came from Ice Man. But the wind only made the fire blaze brighter. Then a light rain began to fall, but the drops seemed only to make the fire hotter with scalding steam. Then the shower turned into a heavy sleet storm that smothered the blaze but made clouds of smoke rise from the red coals.

While the people fled to their houses for shelter, the storm rose to a whirlwind that drove countless flakes of snow into every burning crevice and covered the embers with a white blanket until the fire was dead. Not even a wisp of smoke could be seen in the deep hole.

When at last the storm ended, the people returned and found a lake where the pit had been. Today some people in the Great Smokies say that below the waters of that lake they can hear the sound of coals still crackling.

Ice Man and the Messenger of Springtime
(Chippewa)

Ice Man was sitting in his birch-bark wigwam by the side of a frozen stream. His fire was almost out. He had grown very old and melancholy, and his hair was long and white. He was lonely, and day after day he heard nothing but the howling of winter storms sweeping snow across the land.

One day as his fire was dying to its last orange ember, Ice Man saw a young man approaching his wigwam. The boy's cheeks were red, his eyes shone with pleasure, and he was smiling. He walked with a light and quick step. Around his forehead was a wreath of sweetgrass, and he carried a bunch of flowers in one hand.

"Come in, come in," Ice Man greeted him. "I am happy to see you. Tell me why you come here."

"I am a messenger," replied the young man.

"Ah, then I will tell you of my powers," said Ice Man. "Of the wonders I can perform. Then you shall do the same." From his medicine-bundle, the old man drew out a wonderfully carved pipe and filled it with aromatic leaves. He lighted it with one of the last coals from his dying fire, blew smoke to the four directions, and then handed the pipe to the young stranger.

After the pipe ceremony was concluded, Ice Man said: "When I blow my breath, the streams stand still and the water becomes hard and clear as crystal."

"When I breathe," replied the young man, "flowers spring up all over the land."

"When I shake my long white hair," Ice Man declared, "snow covers the earth. At my command, leaves turn brown and fall from the trees, and my breath blows them away. The water birds rise from the lakes and fly to distant lands. The animals hide themselves from my breath, and the very ground turns as hard as flint."

The young man smiled. "When I shake my hair," he said, "warm showers of soft rain fall upon the earth. The plants lift themselves with delight. My breath unlocks the frozen streams. With my voice I call back the birds, and wherever I walk in the forests their music fills the air." As he spoke, the sun rose higher in the sky and a gentle warmth came over the place. Ice Man sat silent, listening to a robin and a bluebird singing on top of his wigwam. Outside, the streams began to trickle, and the fragrance of flowers drifted on the soft spring breeze.

The young man looked at Ice Man and saw tears flooding from his eyes. As the sun warmed the wigwam, the old man became smaller and smaller, and gradually melted completely away. Nothing remained of his fire. In its place was a small white flower with a pink border, the wild portulaca. People would call it Spring Beauty because it is among the first plants to signal the end of winter and the beginning of springtime.

IV

First Contacts with Europeans

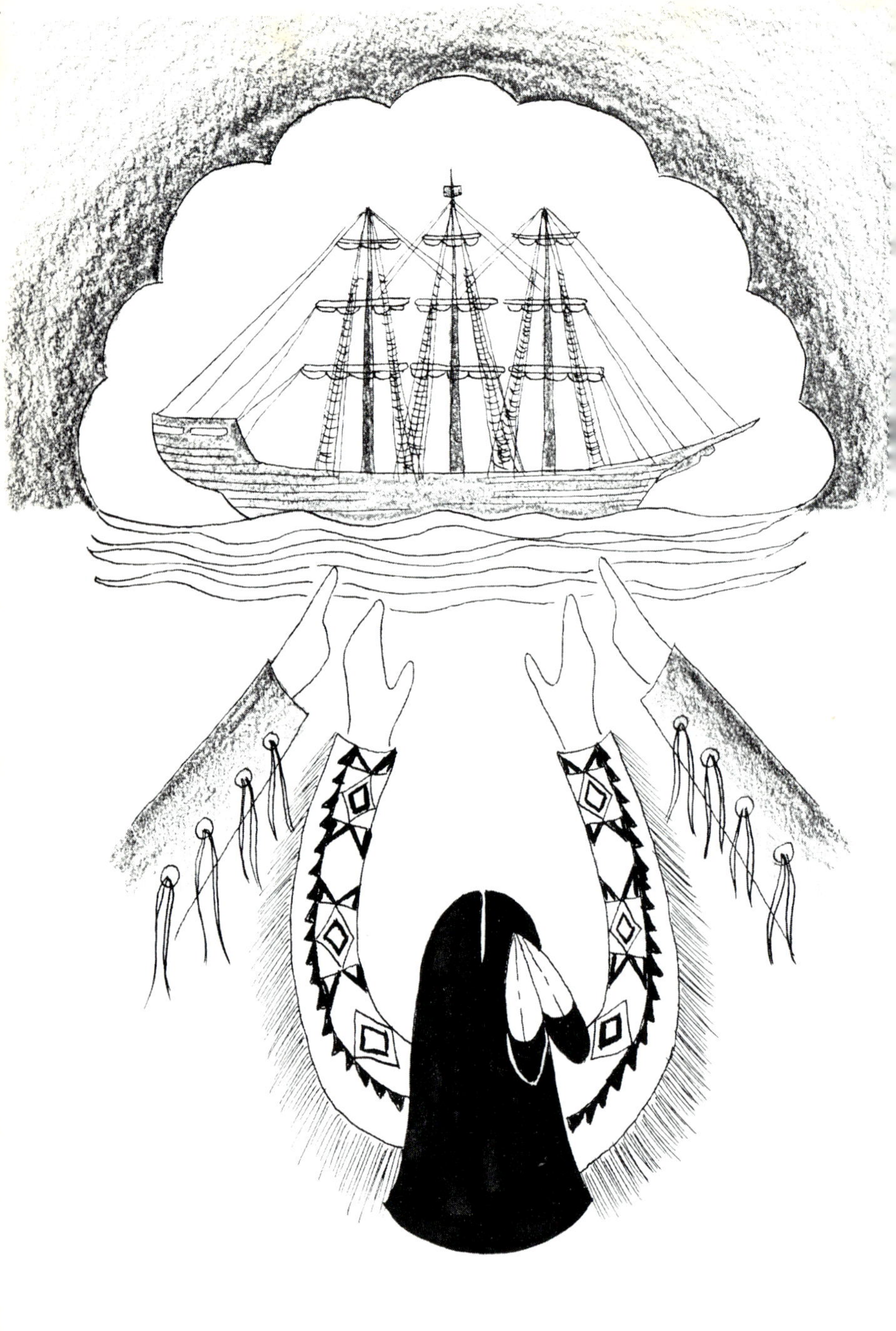

Most American Indian tribes have at least one legend based upon the first time they met light-skinned people from Europe, and the following three stories are representative of all. Through many years of telling and re-telling in the oral tradition of the tribes, the stories have achieved a mythical quality and may bear but slight resemblance to actual events.

It was not unusual for the first explorers along the Atlantic Coast to take Indians back to Europe, either by force or trickery. Whether the incidents in Ioscoda's story happened to Ottawas—who would have had to travel a long distance to the coast—or to young men of a more easterly tribe, we do not know. The story could have been passed from one tribe to another. The tale of Katlian and the Iron People is based upon recorded incidents that occurred when Alexander Baranoff attempted to establish a Russian trading post in Alaska early in the nineteenth century, but the Russian account differs considerably from the Tlingit story. The Cheyenne legend of the coming of the first white man was surely handed down from the days of the first French fur traders. In connection with this it might be useful to read the warning of the Cheyenne prophet, Motzeyouf (pp. 55-57) which evidently went unheeded on that summer's day when a starving trapper stumbled into the Cheyenne camp beyond the Missouri River.

How Ioscoda and His Friends Met the White Men from the East and Journeyed Across the Great Waters
(Ottawa)

One morning before sunrise, Ioscoda and five of his young friends left their Ottawa village and went out hunting with bows and arrows. They passed through a forest and reached the top of a high ridge just as the sun rose out of the east. The air was so clear that the sun appeared to be only a short distance from them.

"How very near the sun is," said one of the boys.

"It cannot be far," Ioscoda agreed. "If you will go with me, we will try to find the place where the sun sleeps."

"Yes, yes," they all said eagerly. Even the youngest of the boys wanted to go on the journey.

"You are too young," they told him.

"If you don't let me go with you," replied the youngest boy, "I will tell your families what you are planning to do."

"You may go with us," said Ioscoda, "but say nothing of this to anyone."

For several days they made preparations for the journey. Each boy collected arrows, supplies of dried meat, extra pairs of moccasins, and as many pieces of tanned hide clothing as he could. They found a dry place deep in the forest and concealed these things there. They also used the place to meet in council and make their plans.

At last they were ready for their quest. On the morning they chose to start, each boy left the village in a different direction, but they soon met at their secret place in the forest. They packed their things on their backs and started toward the east.

Day after day they marched, and each morning as soon as they awakened they faced toward the rising sun, yet it always seemed to be the same distance away from them. Some were discouraged and wanted to turn back, but Ioscoda was confident. "If we keep traveling toward the east," he said, "we shall reach the home of the sun, some time or other."

One morning they found a film of ice along the edge of the stream where they had camped for the night. "Cold weather is coming," said the youngest boy, "and we have no more dried meat. I think we should build a lodge for the winter and spend our time hunting."

Ioscoda would not hear of this. "We will stop only long enough to kill a deer," he replied. "Then we must march on toward the sun's rising."

The next day they came to a large river which flowed eastward, and they followed along its bank. Late one afternoon they reached a rising slope of sand, and as they climbed up through a grove of gnarled and wind-blown trees they saw a vast expanse of blue. They had come suddenly upon an immense body of water. No land could be seen as far as the horizon.

Two of the boys lay down on the beach to drink. As soon as they sucked the water into their mouths, they spat it out. "Salt water!" one of them cried. They had come to the edge of a Great Ocean.

They camped on the beach for the night, and when they awakened at dawn they saw the sun rise as though it had come out of the deep waters. To their great disappointment it appeared to be as far away from them as ever. Before breaking camp, they held council to decide whether to turn back homeward.

"It is true," Ioscoda said, "that the sun's home is beyond this great water, but let us not abandon our quest. If we walk around the shore, surely we will find the place." They all agreed to continue, and he led them northward until they came to the mouth of the wide river they had followed toward the east. "We must build a boat," Ioscoda said. They made camp and gathered as much wood as they could until darkness fell.

Ioscoda spent a restless night, and the next morning he told his companions that a Manito, a good spirit, had come to him in a dream. "The Manito told me that we must go south. Only a short distance beyond the place where we camped on the beach is a river with high banks. We must go there and keep watch off its mouth until we see an island moving in the Great Ocean. The Manito told me that the island would come to us, and that if we get on it, the island will take us toward the sun's rising place."

The boys retraced their footsteps, and by late evening reached a high bluff beyond which they found a river flowing into the ocean. They camped, and next morning watched the sun rise again from the water. "We shall wait here for the island," Ioscoda said. "Yes," one of his friends replied sceptically. "We shall see if that which was said to you in your dream will come true." Ioscoda climbed up to the highest point and kept his eyes fixed on the sea. About midday he called out: "There it is! There it is!"

They all rushed up to join him, and they saw something that might be an island steadily advancing toward the mouth of the river. As it came nearer they could see strangely dressed beings moving about on it. "That is a bad Manito!" the youngest boy cried. "Let us run back into the woods."

"No, no," Ioscoda answered quickly. "Stay and watch."

They saw something splash into the water beside the island, and then it came to a stop. It was close enough now for them to see three trees standing in a row along its surface. The trees were bare of bark and instead of leaves huge pieces of cloth hung from their sides.

A small boat was now lowered from one side, and as it approached the beach, they could see flat sticks moving on each side of it like the flapping of a loon's wings in calm air. The boat entered the mouth of the river.

Some of the boys started to run away. "Come back!" Ioscoda shouted. "We can hide in this hollow place in the rocks. We must see what this can be."

Soon after they crouched down in the hole, they heard the sounds of chopping and then the crash of a falling tree. They heard the crunch of footsteps, and suddenly a man appeared against the sky above them. His skin was light, and hair grew on the lower part of his face. He wore a strange hat and clothing such as they had never seen, and he was gazing down at them. They stared back at him in amazement.

After a few moments the stranger stepped forward, extending

his open hand toward them. Ioscoda took it, and they shook hands. The man spoke and Ioscoda replied, but they could not understand each other's words. Then the man turned and called to his comrades. Several other men in strange clothing came up. They laughed and talked, but the boys could not understand what they were saying.

Finding it impossible to communicate by words, the strangers motioned toward the small boat and the large boat, which Ioscoda and his friends had thought was an island. The men made beckoning signs as if they wanted the boys to come with them.

"Let's go," Ioscoda said quietly. "This is as the Manito told me it would be."

They followed the strangers down to their small boat, which had been loaded with wood, and soon they were bouncing over the waves to the large vessel. The men called it a ship. As the boat came alongside, dozens of strange faces peered down at them. One spoke out, louder than the others, and he seemed to be their leader. He motioned to the boys to climb the rope ladder. As soon as they were on deck, this man whom the others called Captain led them down a ladder to a cabin and gave them some food. He treated them very kindly.

Afterwards they returned to the deck and found the sails all spread above their heads and the ship moving rapidly over the water. The land they had left was fast disappearing in the distance. That night and on the following day Ioscoda and most of his friends were made ill by the motion of the ship, but they soon recovered. As the days passed, they learned to understand and to say a few of the words used by the strangers, and the boys taught them some of the words of the Ottawa people.

One day a man on one of the high masts—that the boys had first thought were trees—cried out in a loud voice: "Land! Land!" Soon after that the Captain took them to a cabin and showed them some clothing similar to that which he wore. He made signs to them to change their worn leather clothing for the other. Ioscoda knew enough of the Captain's language to ask him why they must do this. "To cover your nakedness," the Captain replied, and pointed to their bare legs. "We are coming to my country, and my King will be displeased if your bodies are not properly clothed."

As the ship moved up a river, they saw many houses made of stone along the banks. They passed other ships. One of these vessels had flags flying above it and on its deck were several black objects shaped like logs. Suddenly smoke belched from one of the logs and a noise like thunder frightened Ioscoda and his friends.

"Cannon," the Captain explained calmly, and pointed to the big guns along the other ship's deck. "They're saluting our return from a long voyage."

When the ship docked, the Captain took them to a big house nearby, and led them up some steps to a room outfitted with a bed and several other objects strange to them. He brought them food and drink. "You will stay here until morning," the Captain said. "Then I shall take you to see the King."

Ioscoda and his friends slept very little that night. Until darkness fell, they knelt beside the window, looking out at the people passing up and down. From time to time, they would see a huge animal, larger than a moose, its feet pounding on the cobblestones. Sometimes a man would be riding astride one of these hooved animals; others were fastened with leather straps to an object somewhat like a sledge except that it rolled along on wheels.

Next morning the Captain came and took them out to the street and showed them how to get into one of the wheeled sledges. It contained seats and was covered with leather. They rolled along over the cobblestones almost as swiftly as they had traveled on the ship.

After a while the carriage stopped, and two men dressed in bright-colored clothing helped them down in front of the largest house they had ever seen. They followed the two men and the Captain inside, where shining objects hung from above. They were then taken into a large and splendid room where a man was waiting for them in a great chair decorated with many glittering pieces of metal. The Captain addressed this man as King, and Ioscoda guessed that he must be the chief of all these people.

The Captain bowed down before him, and made signs for the

boys to do as he did. "We welcome these young strangers to our land," the King said, and then he spoke rapidly to the Captain. As best Ioscoda could make out, he was asking if the Indians had come of their own will, or had been forced aboard the ship. The Captain assured the King that the boys had come willingly.

"Ah," said the King, "and where did you young men think you were going?"

"We were going to the east," Ioscoda replied, "to find the place where the sun sleeps." By using signs and a few words he had learned, he soon made the King understand.

"To do such a thing is impossible," said the King. "You can never find such a place."

Ioscoda bowed his head for a moment. "My father," he said to the King, "we have come this far on our long journey, and we will continue it. We have given our lives up to this quest."

The King smiled at the boy, and then slapped his hands together and sent one of the men who was wearing clothes of brilliant colors out of the room.

"I beg of you," Ioscoda continued, "not to stop us from continuing our journey."

The King nodded, still smiling until the courtier who had left the room returned with bundles of presents for the boys. The King passed these gifts out to them, remarking that he would like to see them again before they left his country, and then he bade them good day.

That night Ioscoda's friends held council in their room in the inn. "I am ready to return home," said the youngest boy. "My eyes hunger for the green forests and rivers, the animals, and the songs of the birds. I want to see the faces of my people."

Another agreed with him. "We are not suited for places such as this. If we must go through towns of stone filled with countless strangers we will never live to see the home of the sun."

"Our families will believe we have perished in the wilderness," said another. "They will mourn for us."

"I do not wish to abandon the quest," Ioscoda said. "Tomorrow we will go once more to see the chief of these people, the one they call King, and ask his advice."

"He is a kind man," said the youngest boy. "He is a wise man. He said that we can never find the place of the sun."

Ioscoda's face was sad. "Perhaps he is right," he said. "Perhaps not."

The next morning the King received them again in his palace. When Ioscoda asked him to advise them whether to continue their search, the King complimented them upon their bravery and determination and called them young knights. "In a day or two," he said, "one of my ships will set sail for your country. The ship will take you home. That is my advice to you."

Ioscoda glanced at the faces of his companions and he could see the eagerness in their eyes when they understood the King's words. And so Ioscoda yielded. He told the King they would go on the ship.

Several moons later, after the ship landed them at the mouth of the river where they had first met the light-skinned strangers, Ioscoda and his friends made their way over the last ridge and through the last forest into their village. Within a few minutes, the news of their return started a celebration that lasted far into the night. Their families and friends rejoiced, having long given them up for lost, and the tales the young men told of their adventures brought them much fame.

All were happy except Ioscoda. Every morning he arose before daylight and walked to the high ridge to face the east and watch the sun rise out of the earth. Some day, he told himself, he would resume his quest and find the place where the sun sleeps.

Katlian and the Iron People
(Tlingit)

When the Iron People, the Russians, came to Alaska in vessels much larger than canoes, they had weapons that smoked and made noises like thunder. On their vessels they had larger weapons that hurled balls of iron that would smash trees into pieces. Faced with this great power, Katlian the chief of the Tlingits at Sitka gave the Russians all the furs and skins and other property that they demanded.

Although the Iron People would not go away, there was peace for a time between the Tlingits and the bearded strangers. The Tlingits traded skins for the weapons that thundered, and for cartridges, and they learned to kill animals with these weapons brought by the Iron People.

After a while the Iron People built a village of houses across the inlet and brought their families from their land beyond where the sun sets. One day Katlian's nephew visited the village and saw the daughter of one of the Iron People. He fell in love with her. He followed her to the house where she lived and tried to buy her with furs, but the girl's father angrily sent him away. When Katlian's nephew tried to steal the girl, the Iron People killed him.

This nephew was like a son to Katlian, and at the first opportunity the chief killed the son of one of the Iron People. Baranoff, the leader of these people, sent a message to Katlian to surrender himself, or else all the Tlingits at Sitka would be killed by the weapons that smoked and hurled pieces of metal.

Katlian called his people together and they began building walls out of big cedars. They built houses inside these walls, and put flat rocks between the cedars and the walls of the houses. Soon afterwards the Iron People came in a vessel to destroy them. Ten times they fired their large weapons that hurled balls of iron against the wall of cedars and rocks. Baranoff their leader then called out from the ship for Katlian to surrender himself to them, but Katlian replied in a loud voice that he could not do this. The Iron People then fired more shots at the cedar and rock walls.

After they had done this for a while, the Iron People came off the ship in three small boats. They landed on the beach, carrying guns with bayonets. Katlian led his people out to meet them, and while the Iron People were firing by command, the Tlingits shot into them many times. The Tlingits threw out their empty cartridges quickly and shot again. They killed many of the Iron People. Only those who had charge of the boats got back to the ship. Then the war vessel sailed away.

For two moons, the Tlingits worked to strengthen their little fort, and then the Iron People came again in two war vessels. This time they fired at the cedars and rocks from two directions. Baranoff then shouted: "Katlian, are you still alive?"

"Yes," the chief replied. "I am not afraid of the cannon you use against me."

Again the cannon roared, and again the Iron People came to the beach in boats. Once more, Katlian led the Tlingits against the invaders, and this time they killed many of them and took their guns, coats, hats and swords. The two war vessels sailed away.

After some time had passed, the Iron People returned in a small ship flying white flags of truce. Without weapons of any kind, Baranoff came to the beach under a flag of peace. "Katlian," he called, "are you still alive?"

Katlian walked out of the fort. He carried no weapons. "Yes," he replied, "I am still alive. I won. Now it is all right for you to kill me.'

"I bring you presents," Baranoff said. He gave Katlian clothing, food, rum, and cartridges. After that the Iron People did not bother the Sitka Tlingits again.

How the First White Man Came to the Cheyennes
(Cheyenne)

In a summer long ago, the Cheyennes were camped near some lakes beyond the Missouri River. Awakening from their sleep one morning, Red Eagle and his wife saw a strange creature lying in their tepee. The woman was frightened and was about to cry out, but Red Eagle quieted her and went closer to the strange being which was slowly rising to a sitting position. Red Eagle saw that this creature was a man who looked something like a Cheyenne, but he had a white skin and hair on his face and spoke in a strange language.

The man was so thin that he had scarcely any flesh on his bones, and for clothing he wore only moss and grass. He was very near death. Red Eagle gave him something to eat, but at first the man was so weak and exhausted that his stomach would not hold it, yet after a little while he got stronger.

Red Eagle told his wife to keep the presence of the stranger a secret. He feared that some of his tribesmen would kill the man, believing that he might bring them bad luck. A few days later, the chiefs sent a crier through the camp, announcing that the Cheyennes would be moving camp the next day.

Knowing that the stranger could no longer be concealed, Red Eagle revealed his presence. "I have taken him for my brother," he said. "If anyone harms him I will punish them. The Great Spirit must have sent this man to us for a good reason."

And so Red Eagle clothed him, fed him, and led him back to life. After a time the man learned to speak a few words of Cheyenne. He also learned the sign language of the tribe. In this way he was able to tell Red Eagle that he came from the East, the land of the rising sun. "With five other men I started out to trap the beaver. We were on a lake in a boat when the wind came up suddenly, overturned the boat, and drowned all the others. After I struggled ashore, I wandered about, living on roots and berries until all my clothes were worn and scratched off. Half blind, and nearly dead with hunger, I wandered into your camp and fell into your tepee."

For the hundredth time the man thanked Red Eagle for saving his life, and then he continued: "For many days I have watched how hard you and your wife work. To make a fire you must use two sticks. Your wife uses porcupine quills for needles in sewing. She uses stone vessels to cook in, and you use stone knives and stone points for your spears and arrows. You must work hard and long to make these things. My people, who are powerful and numerous, have many wonderful things that the Cheyennes do not have."

"What are these wonderful things?" Red Eagle asked.

"Needles that keep their points forever for your wife to sew with. Sharp knives of metal to cut with, steel to make a fire with, and a weapon that uses a black powder and sends hard pieces of metal straight at any wild game you need to kill. I can bring you these things if you and your people will help me get beaver skins.

My people are fond of beaver fur, and they will give me these wonderful things for you in exchange."

Red Eagle told his tribesmen what the stranger had said, and they collected many beaver skins for him. The skins were loaded on several travois drawn by dogs, and one day the stranger went off toward the rising sun with his dog-train of furs.

Several moons passed, and Red Eagle began to wonder if the stranger would ever return. Then on a bright sunshiny morning, the Cheyennes heard a noise like a clap of thunder near their camp. On a bluff to the east, they saw a man wearing a red cap and red coat. Above his head he lifted a strange weapon that resembled a black stick, and then he shouted a greeting to them in their own language.

As he approached, they recognized him as the stranger who had taken away the beaver skins. He had brought the Cheyennes all the wonderful things he had told about—knives, needles and steel —and he showed the people how to use them. Then he showed them the black powder and hollow iron with which he had made the noise like thunder. And that is how the first white man came to the Cheyennes.

V

The Coming of the Horse

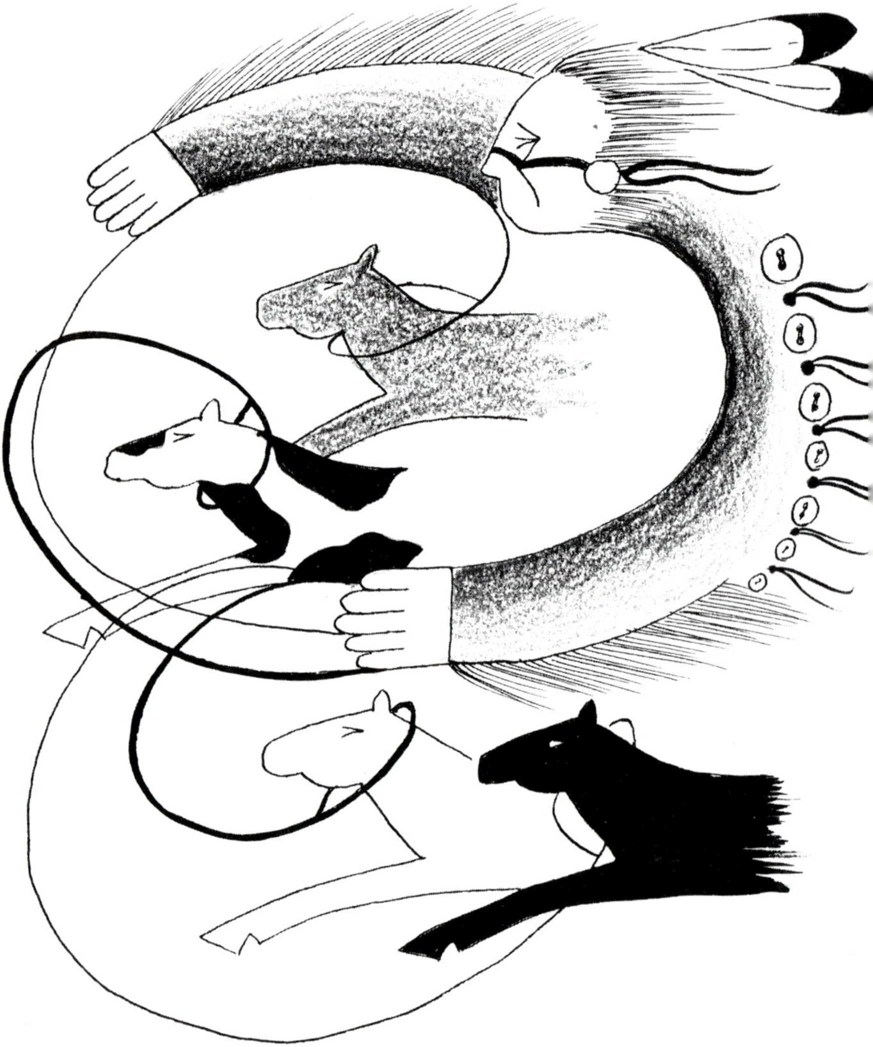

As horses were not acquired by the Indians until after white men brought them from Europe, the stories of that important animal's origins are comparatively recent. The Navahos and Apaches were among the first to obtain horses, and their legends tell of how the Sun and other gods of the Upper World molded them from colored clay and set them loose on earth. Storytellers of the Shoshone and Blackfoot tribes said that the horse was an underwater animal. (They also believed the first white men came from underwater.) According to one myth, the Shoshones captured a Blackfoot woman and tied her to a stake in a dry lake. Shortly afterward a flood filled the lake, and when the water abated there was no woman there, but the lake-bed was filled with horses. The Shoshones caught them, and that is how horses began.

Here are two Blackfoot tales of the origin of horses.

How a Piegan Warrior Found the First Horses
(Blackfoot)

A long time ago a warrior of the Piegan Blackfoot dreamed about a lake far away where some large animals lived. A voice in the dream told him the animals were harmless, and that he could use them for dragging travois and carrying packs in the same way the Indians then used dogs. "Go to this lake," the dream voice told him, "and take a rope with you so that you can catch these animals."

When the Piegan awoke he took a long rope made from strips of a bull buffalo's hide and traveled many miles on foot to the shore of the lake. He dug a hole in the sandy beach and concealed himself there. While he watched, he saw many animals come down to the lake to drink. Deer, coyotes, elk and buffalo all came to quench their thirsts.

After a while the wind began to blow. Waves rose upon the lake and began to roll and hiss along the beach. At last a herd of large animals, unlike any the Piegan had ever seen before, suddenly appeared before him. They were as large as elks, and had small ears and long tails hanging to the ground. Some were white, and some black, and some red and spotted. The young ones were smaller. When they reached the water's edge and bent their heads to drink, the voice the man had heard in his dream whispered to him: "Throw your rope and catch one."

And so the Piegan threw his rope and caught one of the largest of the animals. It struggled and pulled and dragged the man about, and he was not strong enough to hold the animal. Finally it pulled the rope out of his hands, and the whole herd ran into the lake and sank out of sight beneath the water.

Feeling very sad, the Piegan returned to camp. He went into his lodge and prayed for help to the voice he had heard in his dream. The voice answered him: "Four times you may try to catch these animals. If in four times trying you do not catch them, you will never see them again."

Before he went to sleep that night the Piegan asked Old Man

to help him, and while he slept Old Man told him that he was not strong enough to catch one of the big animals. "Try to catch one of the young animals," Old Man said, "and then you can hold it."

Next morning the Piegan went again to the shores of the big lake, and again he dug a hole in the sand and lay hidden there while the deer, the coyotes, the elk and the buffalo came to drink. At last the wind began to rise and the waves rolled and hissed upon the beach. Then came the herd of strange animals to drink at the lake, and again the man threw his rope. This time he caught one of the young animals and was able to hold it.

One by one he caught all the young animals out of the herd and led them back to the Piegan camp. After they had been there a little while, the mares—the mothers of these colts—came trotting into the camp. Their udders were filled with milk for the colts to drink. Soon after the mares came, the stallions of the herd followed them into the camp.

At first the Piegans were afraid of these new animals and would not go near them, but the warrior who had caught them told everybody that they would not harm them. After a while the animals became so tame that they followed the people whenever they moved their camp from place to place. Then the Piegans began to put packs on them, and they called this animal po-no-kah-mita, or elk dog, because they were big and shaped like an elk and could carry a pack like a dog.

That is how the Piegan Blackfoot got their horses.

Water Spirit's Gift of Horses
(Blackfoot)

In the days before horses a poor orphan boy lived among the Blackfoot. Because he was so poor he knew that he could never obtain the things he wanted without the secret power of the gods. One day he left his camp to seek a vision that would tell him what he must do. He slept alone on a high mountain, he prayed near some great rocks, he fasted beside a river, but no vision came to him, no voice spoke to him. He traveled beyond the Sweetgrass Hills to a large lake, and because no sign of any kind had come to him he bowed down and wept.

In that lake lived a powerful Water Spirit, a very old man, and he heard the crying of the poor orphan boy. The Water Spirit sent his young son to find the boy and ask why he was crying. The son went to the weeping boy and told him that his father who lived in the lake wished to see him.

"But how can I go to him if he lives under the lake?" the poor boy asked.

"Hold on to my shoulders and close your eyes," replied the Water Spirit's son. "Don't look until I tell you to do so."

They started into the water. As they moved along, the Water Spirit's son said to the boy: "My father will offer you your choice of the animals in this lake. When he does so, be sure to choose the oldest mallard of the ducks and all its young ones."

As soon as they reached the underwater lodge of the Water Spirit, the son told the boy to open his eyes. He did so, and found himself standing before an old man with long white hair. "Sit beside me," the Water Spirit said, and then asked: "My boy, why do you come to this lake crying?"

"I am a poor orphan," the boy replied. "I left my camp to search for secret powers so that I may be able to make my way in the world."

"Perhaps I can help you," the Water Spirit said. "You have seen all the animals in this lake. They are mine to give to whom I wish. What is your choice?"

Remembering the advice of the Water Spirit's son, the boy replied: "I should thank you for the oldest mallard of the ducks and all its young ones."

"Don't take that one," the Water Spirit said, shaking his head. "It is old and of no value."

But the boy insisted. Four times he asked for the mallard, and then the Water Spirit smiled and said: "You are a wise young man. When you leave my lodge my son will take you to the edge of the lake. After it is dark he will catch the mallard for you. But when you leave the lake don't look back."

The boy did as he was told. The Water Spirit's son gathered some marsh grass from the edge of the lake and braided it into a rope. With this rope he caught the old mallard and led it ashore. He placed the rope in the boy's hand and told him to walk on, but not to look back until sunrise. As the boy walked on toward his camp in the darkness, he heard the duck's feathers flapping on the ground. Later he could no longer hear that sound. Instead he heard the sound of heavy feet pounding on the earth behind him, and from time to time the strange cry of an animal. The braided marsh grass turned into a rawhide rope in his hand. But he did not look back until dawn.

At daybreak he turned around and saw a strange animal at the end of the rope, a horse. A voice told him to mount the animal and he did so, using the rawhide rope as a bridle. By the time he reached camp, he saw many other horses following him.

The people of the camp were frightened by these strange animals, but the boy told them to have no fear. He dismounted and gave everybody horses from the herd that had followed him. There were plenty for everyone, and he had a large number left over for himself.

Until that time, the people had only dogs for carrying their packs and dragging their travois. The boy now showed them how to use the horses for packing, how to break them for riding, and he also gave the horse its Blackfoot name, elk dog. One day the men asked him: "These elk dogs, would they be of any use in hunting buffalo?"

"Yes, let me show you," the boy replied, and as soon as they were mounted he led them out to a buffalo herd where he showed them how to chase buffalo on horseback. He also showed them how to make bridles, saddles, hackamores, whips and other gear for their horses. Once when they came to a river, the men asked him: "These elk dogs, are they of any use to us in water?"

He replied: "That is where they are best. I got them from the water." And he showed them how to use horses in crossing streams.

When the boy grew older, his people made him a chief, and since that time every Blackfoot chief has owned many horses.

VI
Tricksters and Magicians

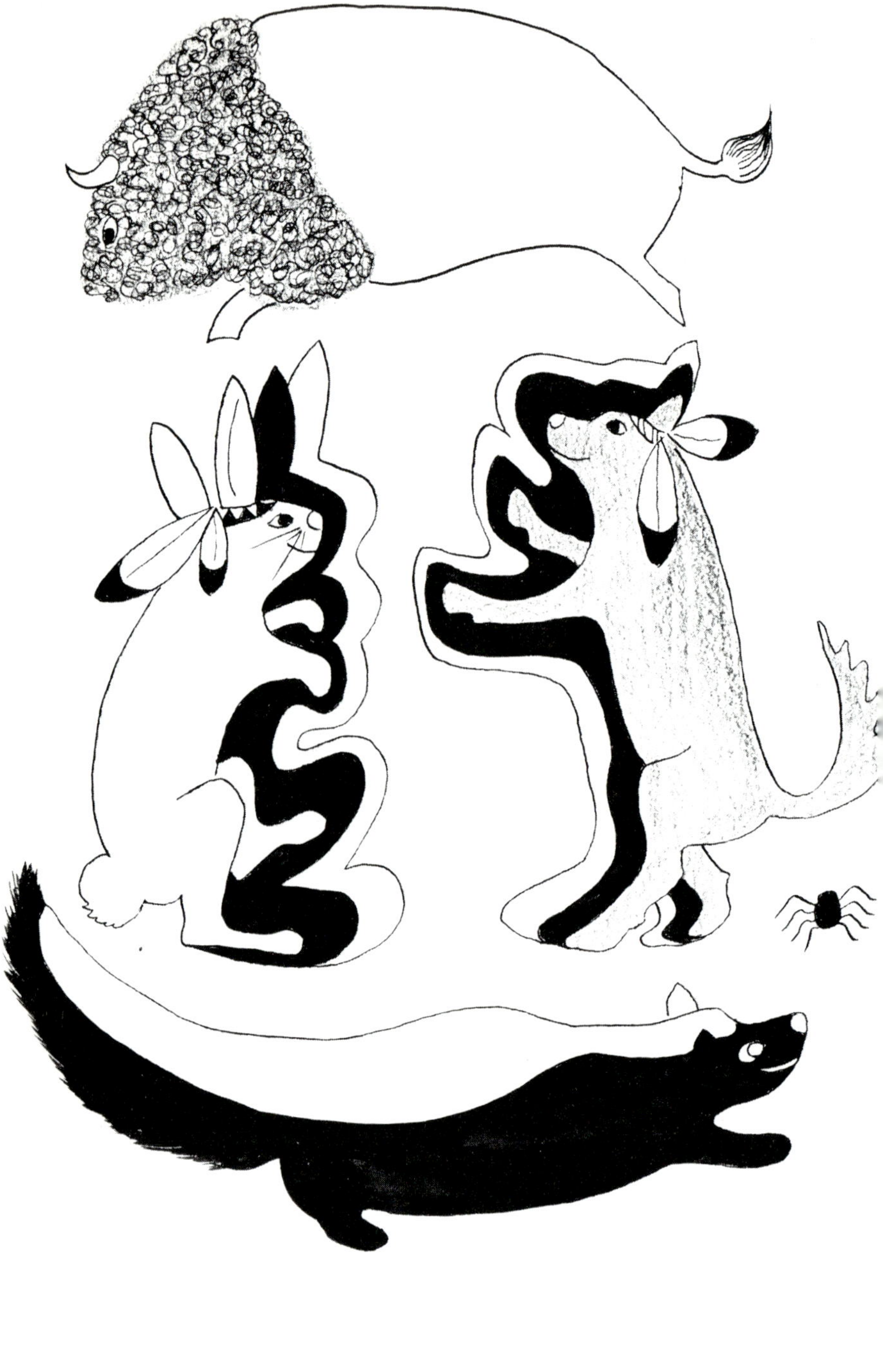

Perhaps the stories most favored by American Indians were those in which a trickster is the central character. In modern terms the trickster was a "confidence man", using his cleverness to outwit the gullible. He made promises only to break them; he presented gifts only to take them back. When his tricks got him into trouble, he escaped through his natural cunning. If the trickster went too far, however, he usually met defeat. The ultimate in trickster stories was a turning of the joke upon the trickster by his intended victim. Yet no matter how difficult a trap the trickster was caught in, he usually escaped in some way to make mischief over and over again in countless other stories.

As will be seen, different tribes have different Tricksters. Rabbit, Wolf and Fox frequently play the part of Trickster, but as we move westward Coyote is more likely to assume this role. Owls, turtles, snakes, bluejays and others were used by some tale tellers, and in the southwest the tarantula was a natural choice. Spiders also appear in many tales, and it may be significant that after the coming of the Europeans to America, the Arapahos used their trickster spider, Nihancan, as a symbol for white men, recognizing them as masters of deception, the greatest tricksters of all.

How Rabbit Fooled Wolf
(Creek)

Two pretty girls lived not far from Rabbit and Wolf. One day Rabbit called upon Wolf and said, "Let's go and visit those pretty girls up the road."

"All right," Wolf said, and they started off.

When they got to the girls' house, they were invited in, but both girls took a great liking to Wolf and paid all their attention to him while Rabbit had to sit by and look on. Rabbit of course was not pleased by this, and he soon said, "We had better be going back."

"Let's wait a while longer," Wolf replied, and they remained until late in the day. Before they left, Rabbit found a chance to speak to one of the girls so that Wolf could not overhear and he said, "The one you've been having so much fun with is my old horse."

"I think you are lying," the girl replied.

"No, I am not. You shall see me ride him up here tomorrow."

"If we see you ride him up here," the girl said with a laugh, "we'll believe he's only your old horse."

When the two left the house, the girls said, "Well, call again."

Next morning Wolf was up early, knocking on Rabbit's door. "It's time to visit those girls again," he announced.

Rabbit groaned. "Oh, I was sick all night," he answered, "and I hardly feel able to go."

Wolf kept urging him, and finally Rabbit said, "If you will let me ride you, I might go along to keep you company."

Wolf agreed to carry him astride of his back. But then Rabbit said, "I would like to put a saddle on you so as to brace myself." When Wolf agreed to this, Rabbit added: "I believe it would be better if I should also bridle you."

Although Wolf objected at first to being bridled, he gave in when Rabbit said he did not think he could hold on and manage to get as far as the girls' house without a bridle. Finally Rabbit wanted to put on spurs.

"I am too ticklish," Wolf protested.

"I will not spur you with them," Rabbit promised. "I will hold them away from you, but it would be nicer to have them on."

At last Wolf agreed to this, but he repeated: "I am very ticklish. You must not spur me."

"When we get near the girls' house," Rabbit said, "we will take everything off you and walk the rest of the way."

And so they started up the road, Rabbit proudly riding upon Wolf's back. When they were nearly in sight of the house, Rabbit raked his spurs into Wolf's sides and Wolf galloped full speed right by the house.

"Those girls have seen you now," Rabbit said. "I will tie you here and go up to see them and try to explain everything. I'll come back after a while and get you."

And so Rabbit went back to the house and said to the girls: "You both saw me riding my old horse, did you not?"

"Yes," they answered, and he sat down and had a good time with them.

After a while Rabbit thought he ought to untie Wolf, and he started back to the place where he was fastened. He knew that Wolf must be very angry with him by this time, and he thought up a way to untie him and get rid of him without any danger to himself. He found a thin hollow log and began beating upon it as if it were a drum. Then he ran up to Wolf as fast as he could go, crying out: "The soldiers are hunting for you! You heard their drum. The soldiers are after you."

Wolf was very much frightened of soldiers. "Let me go, let me go!" he shouted.

Rabbit was purposely slow in untying him and had barely freed him when Wolf broke away and ran as fast as he could into the woods. Then Rabbit returned home, laughing to himself over how he had fooled Wolf, and feeling satisfied that he could have the girls to himself for a while.

Near the girls' house was a large peach orchard, and one day they asked Rabbit to shake the peaches off the tree for them. They went to the orchard together and he climbed up into a tree to shake the peaches off. While he was there Wolf suddenly appeared and called out: "Rabbit, old fellow, I'm going to even the score with you. I'm not going to leave you alone until I do."

Rabbit raised his head and pretended to be looking at some people off in the distance. Then he shouted from the treetop: "Here is that fellow, Wolf, you've been hunting for!" At this, Wolf took fright and ran away again.

Some time after this, Rabbit was resting against a tree-trunk that leaned toward the ground. When he saw Wolf coming along toward him, he stood up so that the bent tree-trunk pressed against his shoulder.

"I have you now," said Wolf, but Rabbit quickly replied: "Some people told me that if I would hold this tree up with the great power I have they would bring me four hogs in payment. Now, I don't like hog meat as well as you do, so if you take my place they'll give the hogs to you."

Wolf's greed was excited by this, and he said he was willing to hold up the tree. He squeezed in beside Rabbit, who said, "You must hold it tight or it will fall down." Rabbit then ran off, and Wolf stood with his back pressed hard against the bent tree-trunk until he finally decided he could stand it no longer. He jumped away quickly so the tree would not fall upon him. Then he saw that it was only a leaning tree rooted in the earth. "That Rabbit is the biggest liar," he cried. "If I can catch him I'll certainly fix him."

After that, Wolf hunted for Rabbit every day until he found him lying in a nice grassy place. He was about to spring upon him when Rabbit said, "My friend, I've been waiting to see you again. I have something good for you to eat. Somebody killed a pony out there in the road. If you wish I'll help you drag it out of the road to a place where you can make a feast off it."

"All right," Wolf said, and he followed Rabbit out to the road where a pony was lying asleep.

"I'm not strong enough to move the pony by myself," said Rabbit, "so I'll tie its tail to yours and help you by pushing."

Rabbit tied their tails together carefully so as not to awaken the pony. Then he grabbed the pony by the ears as if he were going to lift it up. The pony woke up, jumped to its feet, and ran away, dragging Wolf behind. Wolf struggled frantically to free his tail, but all he could do was scratch on the ground with his claws.

"Pull with all your might," Rabbit shouted after him.

"How can I pull with all my might," Wolf cried, "when I'm not standing on the ground?"

By and by, however, Wolf got loose, and then Rabbit had to go into hiding for a long, long time.

Coyote and the Rolling Rock
(Salish-Blackfoot)

One spring day Coyote and Fox were out for a walk, and when they came to a big smooth rock, Coyote threw his blanket over it and they sat down to rest. After a while the sun became very hot, and Coyote decided he no longer needed the blanket. "Here, brother," he said to the rock, "I give you my blanket because you are poor and have let me rest on you. Always keep it."

Then Coyote and Fox went on their way. They had not gone far when a heavy cloud covered the sky. Lightning flashed and thunder rumbled and rain began to fall. The only shelter they could find was in a coulee, and Coyote said to Fox, "Run back to that rock, and ask him to lend us the blanket I gave him. We can cover ourselves with it and keep dry."

So Fox ran back to the rock, and said, "Coyote wants his blanket."

"No," replied the rock. "He gave it to me as a present. I shall keep it. Tell him he cannot have it."

Fox returned to Coyote and told him what the rock had said. "Well," said Coyote, "that certainly is an ungrateful rock. I only wanted the use of the blanket for a little while until the rain stops." He grew very angry and went back to the rock and snatched the blanket off. "I need this to keep me dry," he said. "You don't need a blanket. You have been out in the rain and snow all your life, and it won't hurt you to live so always."

Coyote and Fox kept dry under the blanket until the rain

stopped and the sun came out again. Then they left the coulee and resumed their walk toward the river. After a while they heard a loud noise behind them coming from the other side of the hill. "Fox, little brother," said Coyote, "go back and see what is making that noise."

Fox went to the top of the hill, and then came hurrying back as fast as he could. "Run! run!" he shouted, "that big rock is coming." Coyote looked back and saw the rock roll over the top of the hill and start rushing down upon them. Fox jumped into a badger hole, but the rock mashed the tip of his tail, and that is why Fox's tail is white to this day.

Meanwhile Coyote had raced down the hill and jumped into the river. He swam across to the other side where he was sure that he was safe because he knew that rocks sink in water. But when the rock splashed into the river it began swimming, and Coyote fled toward the nearest woods. As soon as he was deep in the timber, he lay down to rest, but he had scarcely stretched himself out when he heard trees crashing. Knowing that the rock was still pursuing him, Coyote jumped up and ran out on the open prairie.

Some bears were crossing there, and Coyote called upon them for help. "We'll save you," the bears shouted, but the rock came rolling upon them and crushed the bears. About this time Coyote saw several bull buffalo. "Oh, my brothers," he called to them, "help me, help me. Stop that rock." The buffalo put their heads down and rushed upon the rock, but it broke their skulls and kept rolling. Then a nest of rattlesnakes came to help Coyote by forming themselves into a lariat, but when they tried to catch the rock, the rattlesnakes at the noose end were all cut to pieces.

Coyote kept running along a pathway, but the rock was now very close to him, so close that it began to knock against his heels. Just as he was about to give up, he saw two witches standing on opposite sides of the path. They had stone hatchets in their hands. "We'll save you," they called out. He ran between them, with the rock following close behind. Coyote heard the witches strike the rock with their hatchets, and when he turned to look he saw it lying on the ground all shattered into tiny pieces.

Then Coyote noticed that the path had led him into a large

camp. When he sat down to catch his breath, he overheard one of the witches say to the other: "He looks nice and fat. We'll have something good for dinner now. Let's eat him right away."

Coyote pretended he had heard nothing, but he watched the witches through one of his half-closed eyes until they went into their lodge and began rattling their cooking utensils. Then he jumped up and emptied all their water pails.

As soon as they came outside again, he said, "I am very thirsty. I wish you would give me a good drink of water."

"There is plenty of water here," one of the witches replied. "You may have a drink from one of these pails." But when she looked in the pails she found that every one was empty.

"That creek down there has water in it," Coyote said. "I'll go and get some water for you."

He took the pails and started off, but as soon as he was out of sight he ran away as fast as his legs could carry him. Afterwards he heard that when the old witches discovered that he had tricked them, they began blaming each other for letting him escape. They quarreled and quarreled, and fought and fought, until finally they killed each other.

Skunk Outwits Coyote
(Comanche)

Coyote was going along one day, feeling very hungry, when he met up with Skunk. "Hello, brother," Coyote greeted him. "You look hungry and so am I. If I lead the way, will you join me in a trick to get something to eat?"

"I will do whatever you propose," said Skunk.

"A prairie dog village is just over that hill. You go over there and lie down and play dead. I'll come along later and say to the prairie dogs, 'Come, let us have a dance over the body of our dead enemy.'"

Skunk wondered how they would ever get anything to eat by playing dead and dancing. "Why should I do this?" he asked.

"Go on," Coyote said. "Puff yourself up and play dead."

Skunk went on to the prairie dog village and pretended to be dead. After a while Coyote came along and saw several prairie dogs playing outside their holes. They were keeping a distance between themselves and Skunk.

"Oh, look," cried Coyote, "our enemy lies dead before us. Come, we will have a dance to celebrate. Let everyone come out and then stop up the burrow holes."

The foolish prairie dogs did as he told them. "Now," said Coyote, "let us all stand in a big circle and dance with our eyes closed. If anyone opens his eyes to look, he will turn into something bad."

As soon as the prairie dogs began dancing with their eyes closed, Coyote killed one of them. "Well, now," he called out, "let's all open our eyes." The prairie dogs did so, and were surprised to see one lying dead. "Oh, dear," said Coyote, "look at this poor fellow. He opened his eyes and died. Now, all of you, close your eyes and dance again. Don't look, or you too will die."

They began to dance once more, and one by one Coyote drew them out of the dance circle and killed them. At last, one of the prairie dogs became suspicious and opened his eyes. "Oh, Coyote is killing us!" he cried, and all the survivors ran to unstop their holes and seek safety in the burrows.

Skunk then stood up, laughing at how easily Coyote had worked his trick. He helped gather up some dry firewood and they began roasting the prairie dogs that Coyote had killed.

The cooking meat smelled so good that Coyote decided he wanted to eat the best of it himself. "Let's run a race," he said. "The one that wins will have his choice of the most delicious prairie dogs."

"No," replied Skunk, "you are too swift. I'm a slow runner and can never beat you."

"Well, I will tie a rock to my foot," Coyote said.

"If you will tie on a big rock, I will race you."

They decided to race around the bottom of the hill. "While I am tying this rock to my foot," Coyote said, "you go ahead. I'll give you a start and then catch you."

Skunk began to run and was soon out of sight around the hill. Coyote tied a rock to his foot and followed, slowly at first, but he soon kicked the rock loose and doubled his speed. Along the way, however, Skunk had found a brush pile, and he dashed in there and hid.

As soon as he saw Coyote go racing past, Skunk turned back to the fire. He raked all the roasted prairie dogs out of the coals, except for two small bony ones that he did not want. Then he cut off the tails and stuck them back in the ashes, and carried the meat away to the brush pile.

Meanwhile Coyote was still loping around the hill, confident that Skunk was running just ahead of him. As he hurried along, he said to himself, "I wonder where that fool Skunk is? I did not know that he could run so fast." He soon circled back to the cooking fire and saw the prairie dog tails sticking out of the ashes. He seized one and it slipped out. He tried another one. "Oh, but they are well cooked," he said. He tried another one. Then he suspected that something was wrong.

Taking a stick, Coyote raked through the coals, but he found only the two bony prairie dogs that Skunk had rejected. "Someone must have stolen our meat," he said, and then ate the two small tasteless ones.

Skunk, who by this time had feasted on the delicious meat, had crept to the top of the hill and was looking down at Coyote. As Coyote began searching all around to see who might have stolen the meat, Skunk threw some prairie dog bones down upon him.

Coyote glanced up and saw him. "You took all the delicious prairie dogs!" he cried. "Give me some of them."

"No," Skunk answered. "We ran a race for them. I beat you. I'm going to eat all of them."

Coyote begged and begged for some of the delicious prairie dogs, but while he was still pleading, Skunk swallowed the last morsel of meat. He was a better trickster than Coyote.

Nihancan and the Dwarf's Arrow
(Arapaho)

Nihancan the spider was out traveling in search of some mischief he could do to please himself. Along a creek he found a patch of sweet berries, and while he was eating them he heard the sound of someone cutting wood. The sound seemed to come from a grove of cottonwoods across the creek. "I must go over there," Nihancan said to himself. "I have heard that dwarfs who make wonderful arrows live in that place. It is time that I played a trick on them."

He crossed a stream, and among the cottonwoods he found a dwarf making an arrow out of an immense tree that had been cut down. "Well, little brother," said Nihancan, "what are you making?"

"You have eyes to see," replied the dwarf, who continued shaping the tree into an arrow as long as ten men and as thick as a man's body.

"I have heard about your ability to shoot very large arrows," Nihancan said. "But surely you do not expect me to believe that so small a person as you can lift so large a tree. Let me see you shoot it. I will stand over there against that hillside and you can shoot at me."

"I do not want to do that, Nihancan," the dwarf answered, "for I might kill you."

At that, Nihancan laughed and began taunting the dwarf, who remained silent until Nihancan said scornfully: "Just as I thought, you are unable to lift the arrow, and so cannot shoot at me. I shall go on my way."

Then the dwarf said: "I will shoot." Nihancan went toward the hillside and asked in a mocking voice: "Shall I stand here?"

"No, farther away," said the dwarf. "You might get hurt there."

Nihancan went on, and asked again: "Shall I stand here?" But the dwarf continued to tell him to go farther off. At last Nihancan called out: "I will not go any farther. I am as far as your voice reaches." He was now on the hillside, and as he turned to look back he was astonished to see the dwarf pick up the huge tree with one hand.

At once he became frightened and shouted: "Don't shoot at me, little brother. I know you are able to do it. I was only pretending not to believe you."

"Oh, you trickster spider," retorted the dwarf, "I know you are only pretending now. I am going to shoot."

"Please do not shoot!" cried Nihancan, but the dwarf answered him: "I must shoot now. When once I have taken up my bow and arrows I must shoot, or I will lose my power."

Then the dwarf lifted his great arrow and aimed and shot. As Nihancan saw the huge tree coming toward him through the air, he began to yell and run first one way and then another. He did not know where to go, for whichever way he went the arrow turned and headed in the same direction. It continued to come nearer and nearer, its point facing directly toward him. Then he threw himself on the soft ground. The tree struck him and forced him deep into the earth, so that only his head was left outside. He struggled to escape, but the arrow wedged him in.

In a short time the dwarf came up to Nihancan, and after scolding him for doubting his strength, he helped him out and gave him some medicine for his bruises. After that Nihancan went on his way, and he never came back to that place again to play tricks on the dwarfs.

Swift-Runner and Trickster Tarantula
(Zuni)

In the long ago time there was only one Tarantula on earth. He was as large as a man, and lived in a cave near where two broad columns of rock stand at the base of Thunder Mountain. Every morning Tarantula would sit in the door of his den to await the sound of hornbells which signaled the approach of a young Zuni who always came running by at sunrise. The young man wore exceedingly beautiful clothing of red, white and green, a plaited headband of many colors, a plume of blue, red and yellow macaw feathers in his hair knot, and a belt of hornbells. Tarantula was most envious of the young man, and spent much time thinking of ways to obtain his costume through trickery.

Swift-Runner was the young Zuni's name, and he was studying to become a priest-chief like his father. His costume was designed for use in sacred dances. To keep himself strong for these arduous dances, Swift-Runner dressed in his sacred clothing every morning and ran all the way around Thunder Mountain before prayers.

One morning at sunrise, Tarantula heard the hornbells rattling in Swift-Runner's belt. He took a few steps outside of his den, and as the young Zuni approached, he called out to him: "Wait a moment, my young friend, Come here!"

"I'm in a great hurry," Swift-Runner replied.

"Never mind that. Come here," Tarantula repeated.

"What is it?" the young man asked impatiently. "Why do you want me to stop?"

"I much admire your costume," said Tarantula. "Wouldn't you like to see how it looks to others?"

"How is that possible?" asked Swift-Runner.

"Come, let me show you."

"Well, hurry up. I don't want to be late for prayers."

"It can be done very quickly," Tarantula assured him. "Take off your clothing, all of it. Then I will take off mine. Place yours in front of me, and I will place mine in front of you. Then I will put on your costume, and you will see how handsome you look to others."

If Swift-Runner had known what a trickster Tarantula was, he would never have agreed to this, but he was very curious as to how his costume appeared to others. He removed his red and green moccasins, his fringed white leggings, his belt of hornbells, and all his other fine clothing, and placed them in front of Tarantula.

Tarantula meanwhile had made a pile of his dirty woolly leggings, breech-cloth and cape—all of an ugly gray-blue color. He quickly began dressing himself in the handsome garments that Swift-Runner placed before him, and when he was finished he stood up on his crooked hind legs and said: "Look at me now. How do I look?"

"Well," replied Swift-Runner, "so far as the clothing is concerned, quite handsome."

"You can get a better idea of the appearance if I back off a little farther," Tarantula said, and he backed himself, as only Tarantulas can, toward the door of his den. "How do I look now?"

"Handsomer," said the young man.

"Then I'll get back a little farther." He walked backward again. "Now then, how do I look?"

"Perfectly handsome."

"Aha!" Tarantula chuckled as he turned around and dived headfirst into his dark hole.

"Come out of there!" Swift-Runner shouted, but he knew he was too late.

Tarantula had tricked him. "What shall I do now?" he asked himself. "I can't go home half naked." The only thing he could do was put on the hairy gray-blue clothing of Tarantula, and make his way back to the village.

When he reached home the sun was high, and his father was anxiously awaiting him. "What happened?" his father asked. "Why are you dressed in that ugly clothing?"

"Tarantula who lives under Thunder Mountain tricked me," Swift-Runner replied. "He took my sacred costume and ran away into his den."

His father shook his head sadly. "We must send for the warrior-chief," he said. "He will advise us what we must do about this."

When the warrior-chief came, Swift-Runner told him what had happened. The chief thought for a moment, and said: "Now that Tarantula has your fine costume, he is not likely to show himself far from his den again. We must dig him out."

And so the warrior-chief sent runners through the village, calling all the people to assemble with hoes, digging sticks, and baskets. After the Zunis gathered with all these things, the chief led the way out to the den of Tarantula.

They began tunneling swiftly into the hole. They worked and worked from morning till sundown, filling baskets with sand and throwing it behind them until a large mound was piled high. At last they reached the solid rock of the mountain, but they found no trace of Tarantula. "What more can we do?" the people asked. "Let us give up because we must. Let us go home." And so as darkness fell, the Zunis returned to their village.

That evening the leaders gathered to discuss what they must do next to recover Swift-Runner's costume. Someone suggested that they send for the Great Kingfisher. "He is wise, crafty, and swift of flight. If anyone can help us, the Great Kingfisher can."

"That's it," they agreed. "Let's send for the Kingfisher."

Swift-Runner set out at once, running by moonlight until he reached the hill where Great Kingfisher lived, and knocked on the door of his house.

"Who is it?" called Kingfisher.

"Come quickly," Swift-Runner replied. "The leaders of our village seek your help."

And so Kingfisher followed the young man back to the Zuni council. "What is it that you need of me?" he asked.

"Tarantula has stolen the sacred garments of Swift-Runner," they told him. "We have dug into his den to the rock foundation of Thunder Mountain, but we can dig no farther, and know not what next to do. We have sent for you because of your power and ability to snatch anything, even from underwater."

"This is a difficult task you place before me," said Kingfisher. "Tarantula is exceedingly cunning and very sharp of sight. I will do my best, however, to help you."

Before sunrise the next morning, Kingfisher flew to the two columns of rock at the base of Thunder Mountain and concealed himself behind a stone so that only his beak showed over the edge. As the first streaks of sunlight came over the rim of the world, Tarantula appeared in the entrance of his den. With his sharp eyes he peered out, looking all around until he sighted Kingfisher's bill. "Ho, ho, you skulking Kingfisher!" he cried.

At the instant he knew he was discovered, Kingfisher opened his wings and sped like an arrow on the wind, but he merely brushed the tips of the plumes on Tarantula's head before the trickster jumped back deep into his hole. "Ha, ha!" laughed Tarantula. "Let's have a dance and sing!" He pranced up and down in his cave, dancing a tarantella on his crooked legs, while outside the Great Kingfisher flew to the Zuni village and sadly told the people: "No use! I failed completely. As I said, Tarantula is a crafty, keen-sighted old fellow. I can do no more."

After Kingfisher returned to his hill, the leaders decided to send for Great Eagle, whose eyes were seven times as sharp as the eyes of men. He came at once, and listened to their pleas for help. "As Kingfisher, my brother, has said, Tarantula is a crafty, keen-sighted creature. But I will do my best."

Instead of waiting near Thunder Mountain for sunrise, Eagle perched himself a long distance away, on top of Badger Mountain. He stood there with his head raised to the winds, turning first one eye and then the other on the entrance to Tarantula's den until the old trickster thrust out his woolly nose. With his sharp eyes, Tarantula soon discovered Eagle high on Badger Mountain. "Ho, you skulking Eagle!" he shouted, and Eagle dived like a hurled stone straight at Tarantula's head. His wings brushed the trickster, but when he reached down his talons he clutched nothing but one of the plumes on Tarantula's headdress, and even this fell away upon the rocks. While Tarantula laughed and danced in his cave and told himself what a clever well-dressed fellow he was, the shamed and disappointed Eagle flew to the Zuni council and reported his failure.

The people next called upon Falcon to help them. After he heard of what already had been done, Falcon said: "If my brothers, Kingfisher and Eagle, have failed, it is almost useless for me to try."

"You are the swiftest of the feathered creatures," the leaders answered him. "Swifter than Kingfisher and as strong as Eagle. Your plumage is speckled gray and brown like the rocks and sagebrush so that Tarantula may not see you."

Falcon agreed to try, and early the next morning he placed himself on the edge of the high cliff above Tarantula's den. When the sun rose he was almost invisible because his gray and brown feathers blended into the rocks and dry grass around him. He kept a close watch until Tarantula thrust out his ugly face and turned his eyes in every direction. Tarantula saw nothing, and continued to poke himself out until his shoulders were visible. At that moment Falcon dived, and Tarantula saw him, too late to save the macaw plumes from the bird's grasping claws.

Tarantula tumbled into his den, sat down, and bent himself double with fright. He wagged his head back and forth, and sighed: "Alas, alas, my beautiful headdress is gone. That wretch of a falcon! But what is the use of bothering about a miserable bunch of macaw feathers, anyway? They get dirty and broken, moths eat them, they fade. Why trouble myself about a worthless thing like that? I still have the finest costume in the Valley—handsome leggings and embroidered shirt, necklaces worth fifty such head-plumes, and earrings worth a handful of such necklaces. Let Falcon have the old head-plumes."

Meanwhile, Falcon, cursing his poor luck, took the feathers back to the Zunis. "I'm sorry, my friends, this is the best I could do. May others succeed better."

"You have succeeded well," they told him. "These plumes from the South are precious to us."

Then the leaders gathered in council again. "What more is there to be done?" Swift-Runner's father asked.

"We must send your son to the land of the gods," said the war-chief. "Only they can help us now."

They called Swift-Runner and said to him: "We have asked the wisest and swiftest and strongest of the feathered creatures to help us, yet they have failed. Now we must send you to the land of the gods to seek their help."

Swift-Runner agreed to undertake the dangerous climb to the top of Thunder Mountain where the two war-gods, Ahaiyuta and Matsailema, lived with their grandmother. For the journey, the priest-chiefs prepared gifts of their most valuable treasures. Next morning, Swift-Runner took these with him and by midday he reached the place where the war-gods lived.

He found their grandmother seated on the flat roof of their house. From the room below came the sounds of the war-gods playing one of their noisy games. "Enter, my son," the grandmother greeted Swift-Runner, and then she called to Ahaiyuta and Matsailema: "Come up, my children, both of you, quickly. A young man has come bringing gifts."

The war-gods, who were small like dwarfs, climbed to the roof and the oldest said politely: "Sit down and tell us the purpose of your visit. No stranger comes to the house of another for nothing."

"I bring you offerings from our village below. I also bring my burden of trouble to listen to your counsel and implore your aid."

He then told the war-gods of his misfortunes, of how Tarantula had stolen his sacred clothing, and of how the wisest and swiftest of the feathered beings had tried and failed to regain them.

"It is well that you have come," said the youngest war-god. "Only we can outwit the trickster Tarantula. Grandmother, please bestir yourself, and grind some rock flour for us."

While Swift-Runner watched, the old grandmother gathered up some white sandstone rocks, broke them into fragments, and then ground them into a powder. She made dough of this with water, and the two war-gods, with amazing skill, molded the dough into two deer and two antelope which hardened as quickly as they finished their work.

They gave the figures to Swift-Runner and told him to place them on a rock shelf facing the entrance to Tarantula's den. "Old Tarantula is very fond of hunting. Nothing is so pleasing to him as to kill wild game. He may be tempted forth from his hiding-place. When you have done this, go home and tell the chiefs that they should be ready for him in the morning."

That evening after Swift-Runner returned to his village and told how he had placed the figures of deer and antelope on the rock shelf in front of Tarantula's den, the chiefs summoned the warriors and told them to make ready for the warpath before sunrise. All night long they prepared their arrows and tested the strength of their bows, and near dawn they marched out to Thunder Mountain. Swift-Runner went ahead of them, and when he approached the rock shelf, he was surprised to see that the two antelope and the two deer had come to life. They were walking about, cropping the tender leaves and grass.

"I call upon you to help me overcome the wicked Tarantula," he prayed to the animals. "Go down close to his den, I beg you, that he may be tempted forth at the sight of you."

The deer and antelope obediently started down the slope toward Tarantula's den. As they approached the entrance, Tarantula sighted them. "Ho! What do I see?" he said to himself. "There go some deer and antelope. Now for a hunt. I might as well get them as anyone else."

He took up his bow, slipped the noose over the head of it, twanged the string, and started out. But just as he stepped forth from his den, he said to himself: "Good heavens, this will never do! The Zunis will be after me if I go out there." He looked up and down the valley. "Nonsense! There's no one about." He leaped out of his hole and hurried toward the deer, which were still approaching. When the first one came near he drew back an arrow and let fly. The deer dropped at once. "Aha!" he cried. "Who says I am not a good hunter?" He whipped out another arrow and shot the second deer. With loud exclamations of delight, he then felled the two antelope.

"What fine game I have bagged today," he said. "Now I must take the meat into my den." He untied a strap which he had brought along and with it he lashed together the legs of the first deer he had shot. He stooped, raised the deer to his back, and was about to rise with the burden and start for his den, when *cachunk!* he fell down almost crushed under a mass of white rock. "Mercy!" he cried. "What's this?" He looked around but could see no trace of the deer, nothing but a shapeless mass of white rock.

"Well, I'll try this other one," he said, but he had no sooner lifted the other deer to his back when it knocked him down and turned into another mass of white rock. "What can be the matter?" he cried.

Then he tried one of the antelope and the same thing happened again. "Well, there is one left anyway," he said. He tied the feet of the last animal and was about to lift it when he heard a great shouting of many voices.

He turned quickly and saw all the Zunis of the village gathering around his den. He ran for the entrance as fast as his crooked legs would move, but the people blocked his way. They closed in upon him, they clutched at his stolen garments, they pulled earrings from his ears, until he raised his hands and cried: "Mercy! Mercy! You hurt! You hurt! Don't treat me so! I'll be good hereafter. I'll take this costume off and give it back to you without making the slightest trouble if you will only let me alone." But the people closed in angrily. They pulled him about and stripped off Swift-Runner's costume until Tarantula was left unclothed and so bruised that he could hardly move.

Then the chiefs gathered around, and one of them said: "It will not be well if we let this trickster go as he is. He is too big and powerful, too crafty. To rid the world of Tarantula forever, he must be roasted!"

And so the people piled dry firewood into a great heap, drilled fire from a stick, and set the wood to blazing. They threw the struggling trickster into the flames, and he squeaked and sizzled and hissed and swelled to enormous size. But Tarantula had one more trick left in his bag. When he burst with a tremendous noise, he threw a million fragments of himself all over the world—to Mexico and South America and as far away as Taranto in Italy. Each fragment took the shape of Old Tarantula, but of course they were very much smaller, somewhat as tarantulas are today. Some say that Taranto took its name from the tarantulas, some say the tarantulas took their name from Taranto, but everybody knows that the wild dance known as the tarantella was invented by Tarantula, the trickster of Thunder Mountain, in the land of the Zunis.

Buffalo Woman, A Story of Magic
(Caddo)

Snow Bird, the Caddo medicine man, had a handsome son. When the boy was old enough to be given a man's name, Snow Bird called him Braveness because of his courage as a hunter. Many of the girls in the Caddo village wanted to win Braveness as a husband, but he paid little attention to any of them.

One morning he started out for a day of hunting, and while he was walking along looking for wild game, he saw someone ahead of him sitting under a small elm tree. As he approached, he was surprised to find that the person was a young woman, and he started to turn aside.

"Come here," she called to him in a pleasant voice. Braveness went up to her and saw that she was very young and very beautiful.

"I knew you were coming here," she said, "and so I came to meet you."

"You are not of my people," he replied. "How did you know that I was coming this way?"

"I am Buffalo Woman," she said. "I have seen you many times before, from afar. I want you to take me home with you and let me stay with you."

"I can take you home with me," Braveness answered her, "but you must ask my parents if you can stay with us."

They started for his home at once, and when they arrived there Buffalo Woman asked Braveness's parents if she could stay with them and become the young man's wife. "If Braveness wants you for his wife, we will be pleased," said Snow Bird, the medicine man. "It is time that he had someone to love."

And so Braveness and Buffalo Woman were married in the custom of the Caddo people and lived happily together for several moons. One day she asked him, "Will you do whatever I may ask of you, Braveness?"

"Yes," he replied, "if what you ask is not unreasonable."

"I want you to go with me to visit my people."

Braveness said that he would go, and the next day they started for her home, she leading the way. After they had walked a long distance they came to some high hills, and all at once she turned round and looked at Braveness and said: "You promised me that you would do anything I say."

"Yes," he answered.

"Well," she said, "my home is on the other side of this high hill. I will tell you when we get to my mother. I know there will be many coming there to see who you are, and some may provoke you and try to make you angry, but do not allow yourself to become angry with any of them. Some may try to kill you."

"Why should they do that?" asked Braveness.

"Listen to what I am about to tell you," she said. "I knew you before you knew me. Through magic I made you come to me that first day. I said that some will try to make you angry, and if you show anger at even one of them, the others will join in fighting you until they have killed you. They will be jealous of you. The reason is that I refused many who wanted me."

"But you are now my wife," Braveness said.

"I have told you what to do when we get there," Buffalo Woman continued. "Now I want you to lie down on the ground and roll over twice."

Braveness smiled at her, but he did as she had told him to do. He rolled over twice, and when he stood up he found himself changed into a Buffalo.

For a moment Buffalo Woman looked at him, seeing the astonishment in his eyes. Then she rolled over twice, and she also became a Buffalo. Without saying a word she led him to the top of the hill. In the valley off to the west, Braveness could see hundreds and hundreds of Buffalo.

"They are my people," said Buffalo Woman. "This is my home."

When the members of the nearest herd saw Braveness and Buffalo Woman coming, they began gathering in one place, as though waiting for them. Buffalo Woman led the way, Braveness following her until they reached an old Buffalo cow, and he knew that she was the mother of his beautiful wife.

For two moons they stayed with the herd. Every now and then, four or five of the young Buffalo males would come around and annoy Braveness, trying to arouse his anger, but he pretended not to notice them. One night, Buffalo Woman told him that she was ready to go back to his home, and they slipped away over the hills.

When they reached the place where they had turned themselves into Buffalo, they rolled over twice on the ground and became a man and a woman again. "Promise me that you will not tell anyone of this magical transformation," Buffalo Woman said. "If people learn about it, something bad will happen to us."

They stayed at Braveness's home for twelve moons, and then Buffalo Woman asked him again to go with her to visit her people. They had not been long in the valley of the Buffalo when she told Braveness that the young males who were jealous of him were planning to have a foot-race. "They will challenge you to race and if you do not outrun them they will kill you," she said.

That night Braveness could not sleep. He went out to take a long walk. It was a very dark night without moon or stars, but he could feel the presence of the Wind spirit.

"You are young and strong," the Wind spirit whispered to him, "but you cannot outrun the Buffalo without my help. If you lose, they will kill you. If you win, they will never challenge you again."

"What must I do to save my life and keep my beautiful wife?" asked Braveness.

The Wind spirit gave him two things. "One of these is a magic herb," said the Wind spirit. "The other is dried mud from a medicine wallow. If the Buffalo catch up with you, first throw behind you the magic herb. If they come too close to you again, throw down the dried mud."

The next day was the day of the race. At sunrise the young Buffalo gathered at the starting place. When Braveness joined them, they began making fun of him, telling him he was a man-buffalo and therefore had not the power to outrun them. Braveness ignored their jeers, and calmly lined up with them at the starting point.

An old Buffalo started the race with a loud bellow, and at first Braveness took the lead, running very swiftly. But soon the others began gaining on him, and when he heard their hard breathing close upon his heels, he threw the magic herb behind him. By this time he was growing very tired and thought he could not run any more. He looked back and saw one Buffalo holding his head down and coming very fast, rapidly closing the space between him and Braveness. Just as this Buffalo was about to catch up with him, Braveness threw down the dried mud from the medicine wallow.

Soon he was far ahead again, but he knew that he had used up the powers given him by the Wind spirit. As he neared the goal set for the race, he heard the pounding of hooves coming closer behind him. At the last moment, he felt a strong wind on his face as it passed him to stir up dust and keep the Buffalo from overtaking him. With the help of the Wind spirit, Braveness crossed the goal first and won the race. After that, none of the Buffalo ever challenged him again, and he and Buffalo Woman lived peacefully with the herd until they were ready to return to his Caddo people.

Not long after their return to Braveness's home, Buffalo Woman gave birth to a handsome son. They named him Buffalo Boy, and soon he was old enough to play with the other children of the village. One day while Buffalo Woman was cooking dinner, the boy slipped out of the lodge and went to join some other children at play. They played several games and then decided to play that they were Buffalo. Some of them lay on the ground to roll like Buffalo, and Buffalo Boy also did this. When he rolled over twice, he changed into a real Buffalo calf. Frightened by this, the other children ran for their lodges.

About this time his mother came out to look for him, and when she saw the children running in fear she knew that something must be wrong. She went to see what had happened and found her son changed into a Buffalo calf. Taking him up in her arms, she ran down the hill, and as soon as she was out of sight of the village she turned herself into a Buffalo and with Buffalo Boy started off toward the west.

Late that evening when Braveness returned from hunting he could find neither his wife nor his son in the lodge. He went out to look for them, and someone told him of the game the children had played and of the magic that had changed his son into a Buffalo calf.

At first, Braveness could not believe what they told him, but after he had followed his wife's tracks down the hill and found the place where she had rolled he knew the story was true. For many moons, Braveness searched for Buffalo Woman and Buffalo Boy, but he never found them again.

VII
Heroes and Heroines

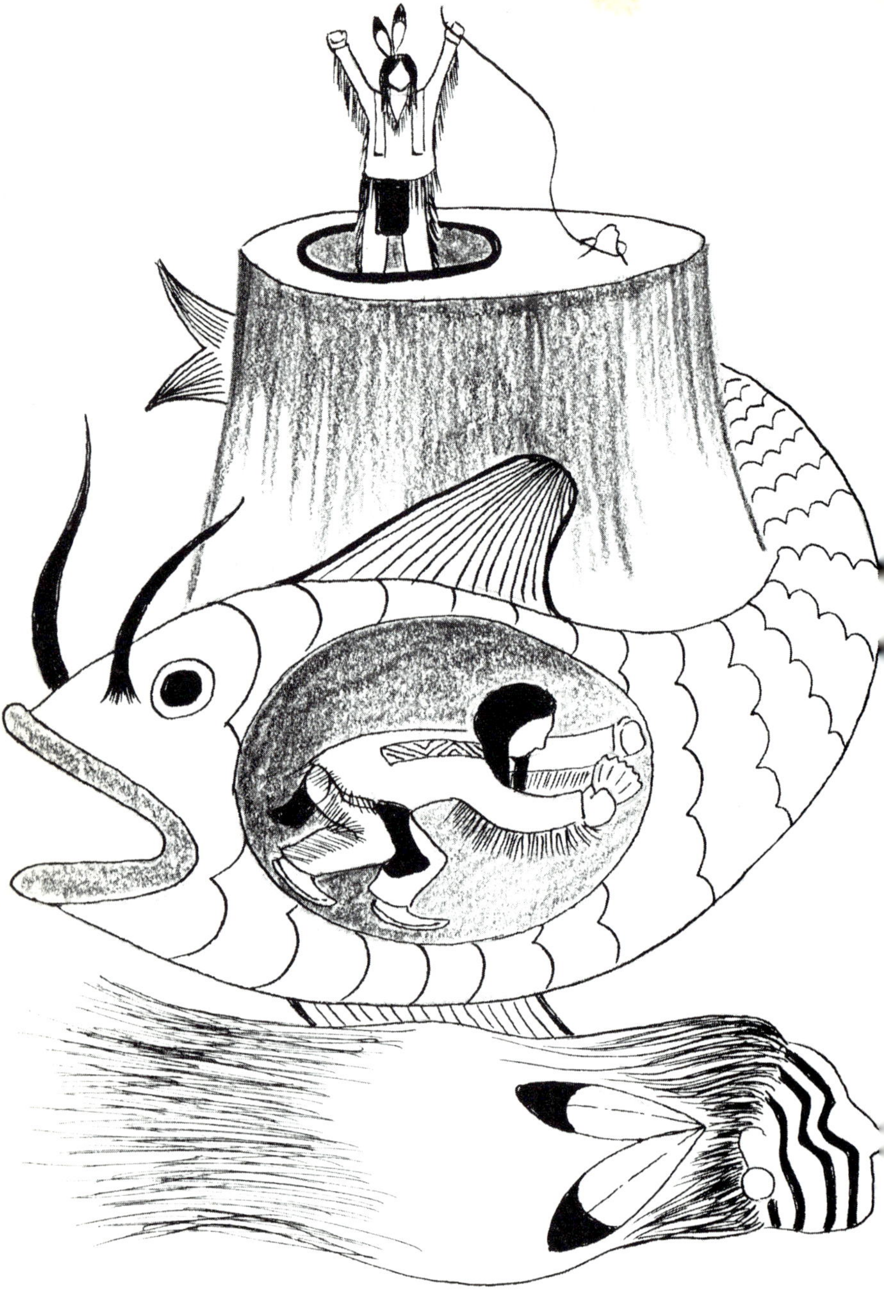

All peoples around the world have their folktales of heroes and heroines. In the three which follow, readers may recognize similarities to stories of other times and other countries. "The Hunter and the Dakwa", for example, is a Cherokee version of the Biblical story of Jonah who was swallowed by a great fish and escaped with his life.

Many stories of heroism are based upon real events in the histories of Indian tribes. "The Prisoners of Court House Rock" was a true incident of Pawnee history in which courage and ingenuity made escape possible for a band of warriors under siege. The romance of "Red Shield and Running Wolf" also must have originated from a series of incidents that occurred during the long and troublous relationship between the Crow and Sioux tribes.

The Hunter and the Dakwa
(Cherokee)

In the old days there was a great fish called the Dakwa which lived in the Tennessee River near the mouth of Toco Creek. This fish was so large that it could easily swallow a man. One day several hunters were traveling in a canoe along the Tennessee when the Dakwa suddenly rose up under the canoe and threw them all into the air. As the men came down, the fish swallowed one with a single snap of its jaws, and dived with him to the bottom of the river.

This man was one of the bravest hunters in the tribe, and as soon as he discovered where he was he began thinking of some way to overcome the Dakwa and escape from its stomach. Except for a few scratches and bruises, the hunter had not been hurt, but it was so hot and airless inside the big fish that he feared he would soon smother.

As he groped around in the darkness, his hands found some musselshells which the Dakwa had swallowed. These shells had very sharp edges. Using one of them as a knife, the hunter began cutting away at the fish's stomach. Soon the Dakwa grew uneasy at the scraping inside his stomach and came up to the surface of the river for air. The man kept on cutting with the shell until the fish was in such pain that it swam wildly back and forth across the river, thrashing the water into foam with its tail.

At last the hunter cut through the Dakwa's side. Water flowed in, almost drowning the man, but the big fish was so weary by this time that it came to a stop. The hunter looked out of the hole and saw that the Dakwa was now resting in shallow water near the riverbank.

Reaching up, the man pulled himself through the hole in the fish, moving very carefully so as not to disturb the Dakwa. He then waded ashore and returned to his village, where his friends were mourning his death because they were sure he had been eaten by the great fish. Now they named him a hero and held a celebration in his honor. Although the brave hunter escaped with his life, the juices in the stomach of the Dakwa had scalded all the hair from his head, and he was bald forever after.

The Prisoners of Court House Rock
(Pawnee)

Far out on the plains of western Nebraska is a towering formation of rock and clay which the early fur traders named Court House Rock because its shape reminded them of the first courthouse in St. Louis. In the years before the white men came, and before wind and rain eroded its shape, Court House Rock was much more difficult to climb or descend. On all sides except one the walls of this rock were smoothed and polished, offering no projecting points to serve as foot or hand holds. Only on one side could a climber reach the flat surface of the rock, and this could be done only by chopping steps into the hard clay with a hatchet or some other sharp tool.

One day during that long ago time a Pawnee hunting party was camped near Court House Rock. Suddenly a large war party of Sioux appeared and surrounded the Pawnees. The Sioux drove them back to the rock, and the Pawnees escaped with their lives by climbing to the top.

Although the Sioux dared not follow the Pawnees up the steep steps, they posted guards at the only place where the Pawnees could come down, and then the remainder of the warriors camped all around the base of the rock to starve the Pawnees into submission.

The Pawnees had little food and no water, and after two or three days they began to suffer terribly from hunger and still more from thirst. Spotted Horse, their leader, suffered most of all because he was responsible for the lives of all the warriors in the hunting party. He did not mind dying himself, but he knew that his memory would be disgraced if he lost the young men that he led.

Every night he went alone to the edge of the rock and prayed to Tirawa the Spirit Chief. One night while he was praying a voice spoke to him out of the darkness: "If you look hard enough you will find a place where you can escape from this rock, and so save all your men and yourself."

At first daylight, Spotted Horse searched all the ledges for a place where it might be possible to descend without the Sioux discovering them. At last he found near the edge of the cliff a knob of soft clay sticking up above the hard rock surface. Looking over the edge, Spotted Horse saw that just below the knob of clay was one of the smooth sides of the rock which had been left unguarded by the Sioux. With his knife he began cutting into the clay, and by nightfall he had carved an open hole as large around as a man's body.

Spotted Horse then called his warriors together and asked them to give him all their lariats. After tying the lariats end to end, he looped the first one around a projecting rock, and dropped down through the hole he had dug. As it was too dark to see whether or not the rope reached the ground, Spotted Horse slowly descended it until his feet touched the earth. All around him he could see the glimmering campfires of the besieging Sioux, and he could hear the distant voices of the guards who were watching the place where the Pawnees had climbed to the summit.

Pulling himself up hand over hand, Spotted Horse soon reached the top of the rock again. Cautioning his warriors to make no sounds during the descent or after they reached the ground, he started them down. He ordered the youngest to go first, then the next youngest, and so on, until last of all came his turn. Then he let himself down, and they all crept through the unsuspecting Sioux camp and escaped.

Spotted Horse and his Pawnee braves never knew for certain how long the Sioux remained in camp around Court House Rock, waiting for them to starve. Very likely the Sioux discovered the dangling lariats the very next morning, and realized that they had been outwitted by a worthy foe.

Red Shield and Running Wolf
(Crow)

In years past the Sioux and the Crows were enemies, and only through heroic action could a young person of one tribe become the friend or lover of a young person of the other tribe. Such was the story of Red Shield, the daughter of a Sioux chief, and Running Wolf, the son of a Crow warrior.

Red Shield first heard of Running Wolf from a Sioux woman who had been captured by the Crows and then later was permitted to return to her people. This woman had lived as a servant with Running Wolf's family during the time when the boy was growing up.

"He was a lazy boy," the Sioux woman told Red Shield. "His father had to drive him out of bed every morning by rapping his shins with a stick. One morning he scolded the boy very hard and told him that he should be out hunting deer for the family. That morning, as soon as the father left the tepee, Running Wolf came to me and asked if I would make a buckskin mask for him. And so I made him a mask, and he spent the day painting it with white clay and fastening deer horns to it. Before sunrise the next morning he was the first one out of bed. He took his father's gun and knife and rode away on a horse, with two led horses behind him. He went out to a little lake near their village, fastened his horses in the woods, and then went down to a place where animals come to drink. When the sun rose some deer came there, but they did not run away because they thought the boy was a deer. He killed two, loaded them on the led horses, and brought them home just as his father was waking up."

"Was Running Wolf's father pleased by this?" Red Shield asked.

"Oh, yes. He told his son that he had done well, and should divide the venison with their neighbors. But that was not the end of it. The next morning the boy went back to the watering-place and returned with two more deer, and the morning after that he did the same." The Sioux woman smiled. "That time his father told him to stop or he would begin to smell like a deer."

"And what did young Running Wolf say to this?"

"He said nothing, but he began sleeping late again, until one morning his father rapped him on the shins and scolded him for being lazy. His father told Running Wolf that he could no longer use the family's horses, that if he wanted a horse to ride he would have to go out and take one from the Nez Perces. That morning, as soon as his father went hunting, Running Wolf came to me and asked if I would make him a new pair of moccasins. I did this for him, and he spent the day decorating them with paint and beads in some special way. At sundown he left the tepee with his gun, not saying a word to anyone. Next morning he returned with twenty horses that he had taken from the Nez Perces."

"His father must have been much pleased by this," said Red Shield.

"Oh, yes, after the boy gave him ten of the horses, the father sang praise songs for him all day. But that was not the end of it. That night Running Wolf went out again, and next morning he brought back forty horses and gave them all to his father. And the next night he captured fifty horses, all of which he gave to his father. And still a fourth night he went and this time he brought back eighty head of horses, giving them all to his father! Oh, I can tell you, Running Wolf's father had a hard time herding all those horses. 'Stop! stop!' he shouted at his son. 'You have listened too well to what I told you.'"

Red Shield laughed. "I think I like this young Running Wolf, even if he is a Crow," she said.

"Oh, but he soon grew up after that," the Sioux woman said. "After his father died, his mother and I made a new tepee for him, and then I was told that I could return to my people. Running Wolf painted his tepee black, tied feathers to the door, and laid war bonnets and other finery around the inside to signify that he intended to become a mighty warrior."

Not long after Red Shield heard these stories about Running Wolf, her father announced that the Sioux would be going out for their summer buffalo hunt. The tribe camped in a narrow valley down which some of their hunters would drive the buffalo while others waited in concealment on either side to kill them as they passed. It was a busy time for Red Shield and the other women, young and old, for they helped in the skinning of the buffalo and then stretched the hides out to dry in the sun.

One afternoon while half the Sioux hunters were out searching for a buffalo herd, an alarm suddenly spread through the camp. "Crow horse thieves are coming! Look to the horses!" As soon as the men drove the horses in, it was the duty of the women and children to guard them while the warriors went out to protect the camp from the Crow raid. Red Shield mounted her spotted pony and joined the other women. Far up the level valley she could see the dust of the oncoming Crows as they raced toward the line of defending Sioux. A moment later she heard the sharp war cries of the contending warriors.

She saw one of the Crow warriors on a black horse break through the Sioux line and come charging toward the horse herd she was helping to guard. Not far behind him, two Sioux warriors galloped in pursuit. As the Crow came nearer she could see that he wore four eagle feathers in his hair. Fastened behind his belt was a streamer of black leather long enough to trail on the ground. His horse's mane and tail were whitened with clay. He carried a black-handled spear decorated with bunches of crow feathers, and this weapon was pointed straight at Red Shield. She held her spotted horse steady, defying the onrushing Crow, and at the last moment he reined in the black horse so that the point of the spear was only an arm's length from her body.

The young Crow's face was painted with streaks of black and white. For a moment he glared at Red Shield, his eyes very bright, and then he threw back his head and laughed. By this time his pursuers had caught up with him. One of the Sioux put an arrow to his bow but missed; then both of them closed in upon the Crow with their war clubs raised, ready to strike.

Dancing his black horse in a circle, the Crow used his spear to knock first one and then the other Sioux off their mounts. His horse pawed the earth, then sprang like a cat into the Sioux horse herd. Before Red Shield or her companions could move, the

Crow had cut six horses out of their herd and was chasing them off down the valley.

Angry and frustrated because she could do nothing to stop the daring Crow, Red Shield watched him go. Then the young man turned and waved a farewell to her. Above the pounding hooves she could hear his laughter, and her indignation turned to grudging admiration.

A group of Sioux warriors swept by intent upon pursuit, but Red Shield's father called them back. "Too many of our hunters are away," he said. "We are too few to risk leaving our women and children and the horse herd open to another raid."

"Did you see that Crow!" cried an old Sioux medicine man. "He and his horse are under some powerful magic."

The Sioux woman who had once been a captive among the Crows spoke up from the front of her tepee. "I know that one," she said.

"What name does he go by?" the medicine man asked.

"Yes, who is he?" demanded Red Shield's father.

"Running Wolf, he is called."

Red Shield, who still sat on her spotted horse, whispered to herself: "Running Wolf! I knew he must be Running Wolf."

Not long after that the Sioux returned to their village on the Missouri River. It seemed to all the young men in the tribe that the chief's daughter, Red Shield, had suddenly become a great beauty, and one by one they came by the chief's tepee to ask if she would marry them. Red Shield's father encouraged her to choose one of the suitors for a husband, but she wanted none of them. One evening after she had rejected a handsome young warrior, her father demanded to know why she was so obstinate.

"Because I do not love him!" she cried, and in a fit of anger she threw her supper into the fire.

"If you love someone else," her father said patiently, "then tell me his name."

"I love only Running Wolf," she replied. "I want to marry him."

"You cannot marry Running Wolf. He is a Crow, and the Crows are our enemies."

Her father thought that would put an end to it, but days passed without Red Shield saying a word, and she ate so little that she began to grow thin. At last he realized that his daughter was determined to marry Running Wolf or else will herself to die.

"Very well," the chief said, "at least you are a woman of courage. You do not know if Running Wolf wants you for a wife, but you are determined to test him."

The next morning the chief brought around two fine horses, a mule, and some packs filled with moccasins and other presents. He summoned the Sioux woman who had once been a captive of the Crows and told her to go with Red Shield until they found the Crow camp where Running Wolf lived. They started out and at the end of three days they sighted the Crow tepees along a little stream. They rode into a thick wood where they fastened their horses and the pack mule. Red Shield painted herself carefully and dressed in her best clothing. By this time night had fallen, but a full moon was rising above the trees.

"It's time for me to go into the Crow camp," Red Shield said.

"Remember to look for a black tepee," the Sioux woman reminded her. "You will see a bunch of eagle feathers fastened to the end of one of the poles."

"If I don't return," Red Shield whispered, "you will know that Running Wolf does not want me for a wife and that I am a prisoner of the Crows as you once were."

"I will wait for you," the Sioux woman said.

Red Shield walked out of the woods and entered the bright moonlight which flooded the Crow camp. In the middle of the camp she found a black tepee with eagle feathers fastened to the top of one of the poles. No one noticed her as she walked to the open entrance.

Inside some young men were talking and smoking around a campfire. Red Shield was certain that one of them was Running Wolf. She sat down outside the entrance. After a while the young men began to leave, one or two at a time, paying no particular attention to her presence.

Then Running Wolf came out to stretch himself and yawn.

The moonlight was full on his face, and Red Shield felt her heart beat strongly. He saw her then, and said in Crow, "Come in," but Red Shield understood not one word of Crow and she neither answered him nor moved. Running Wolf shrugged and went back inside, and Red Shield heard him say something else. The voice of an old woman responded.

Red Shield arose then and went into the tepee. The fire had died to a few coals and she could see only the shadowy forms of Running Wolf and his mother. She went close to the fire and sat down as though to warm herself.

This time the old woman spoke to her in Crow. "Take off your moccasins and rest." But of course Red Shield did not understand. "Build up the fire so that we can see this young woman," said Running Wolf. His mother placed some dry wood on the coals, and a blaze sprang up to light the inside of the tepee.

"This is not a Crow woman!" cried Running Wolf's mother.

"No," he said. "But I know who she is. Only one time have I seen her but her face has been in my dreams many times since. She is Sioux."

Red Shield raised her head, and made signs to tell them she could not understand what they were saying, but that she had a friend nearby who could speak for her. At last Running Wolf understood, and he followed her across the camp clearing into the thick woods where the Sioux woman was waiting with the horses and mule. Running Wolf remembered the former captive of his boyhood, and when they returned to his tepee the Sioux woman and his mother had a happy reunion.

"Why do you and this daughter of a Sioux chief come into our camp?" the mother asked.

"She is Red Shield," replied the Sioux woman. "She has brought many presents. She has come to marry your son, Running Wolf."

"And what does my son, Running Wolf, have to say to this? To marry one of the enemy?"

Running Wolf looked at Red Shield. "I knew she was beautiful, and she showed courage that day I took horses from the Sioux. Now she has shown more bravery than I would have dared, by coming into the camp of her enemies alone. I want her for my wife."

While the Sioux woman was bringing in the packs of presents, Running Wolf's mother went through the camp. "Come and look at my son's wife!" she cried. "One of the enemy's children has come to marry him!" All the Crows in camp came to see Red Shield, and all said she was very good-looking and a young woman of great bravery.

Early the next morning the Sioux woman started back on the long journey to the Missouri River to tell the girl's people that she was safe and was now the wife of the Crow warrior, Running Wolf. A few days later Red Shield's father, the Sioux chief, sent two messengers to the Crow chief, telling him that he and many of his relatives were coming to pay the Crows a friendly visit.

For this event the Crows moved their tepees to a larger plain beside a lake, camping in a tight circle so as to leave room for the visitors. The Crow chief told Running Wolf to put his black tepee in the place of honor in the center. When the Sioux arrived, the Crows surrounded them and watched them put up their tepees. After this was done, Red Shield took Running Wolf to welcome her parents, and they all exchanged many presents. Running Wolf brought several guns and the horses he had taken from the Sioux and gave them to Red Shield's father.

For four days and nights the Sioux camped with the Crows and the tribes danced together every evening. After the Sioux returned to the Missouri River, Running Wolf and Red Shield and several of their friends visited them from time to time, and in the moons of pleasant weather, her Sioux father and mother came to visit their daughter, and later on to see their grandchildren. In both tribes, the young Crow warrior and his Sioux wife were regarded as hero and heroine, and their people lived in peace for a time.

VIII
Animal Stories

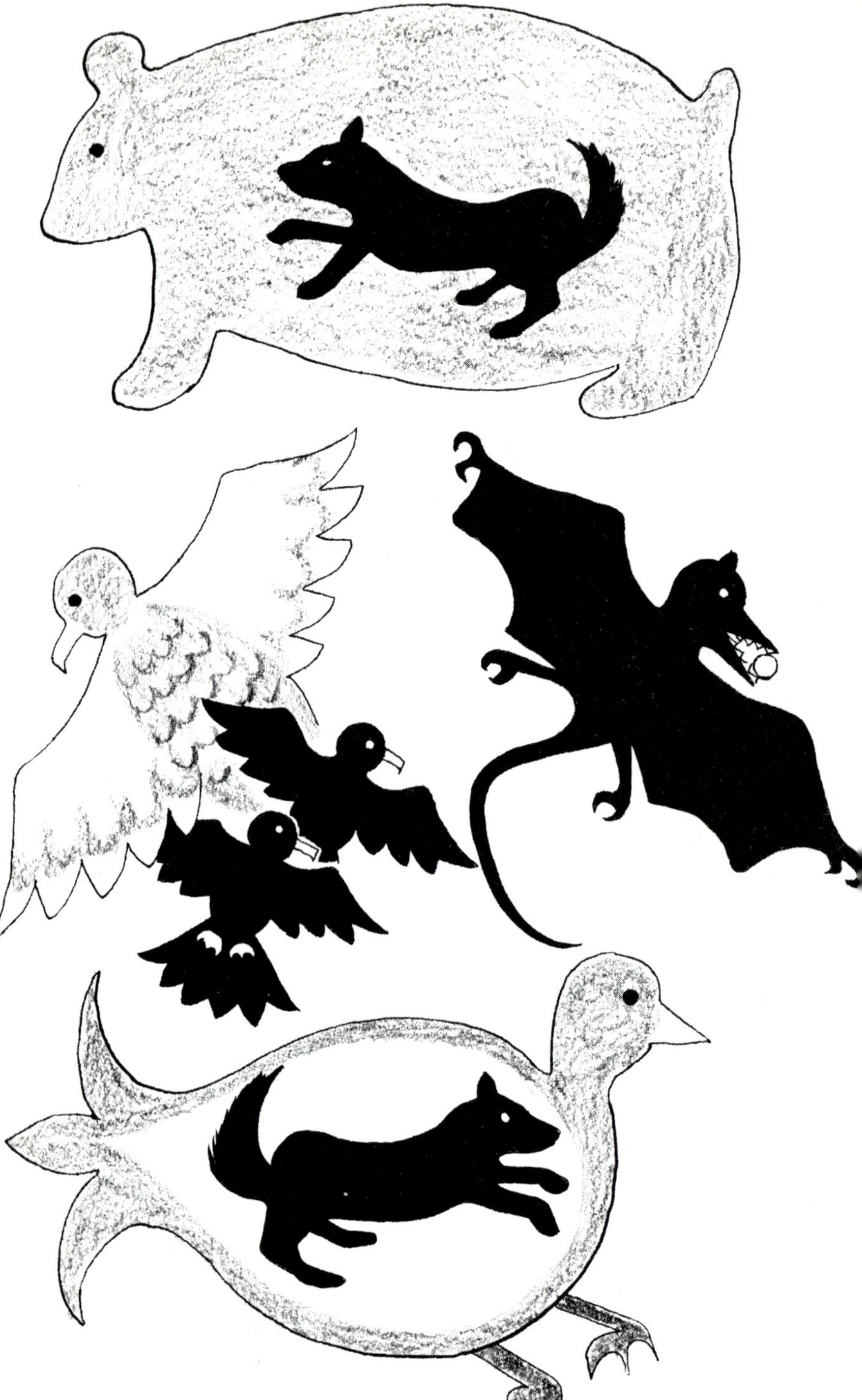

At the beginning of this collection are several stories about animals who play equal roles with human beings. The four tales which follow are animal stories that do not involve people. Among the favorite animal tales of American Indians are those in which weaker or smaller animals outwit the more powerful, or in which rascally tricksters such as Coyote are made to play the fool. Some are humorous, dealing with competitions between rivals. Others demonstrate the rewards of hard work and justice, as in the Cochiti fable, "Crow and Hawk".

The Bluebird and the Coyote
(Pima)

A long time ago the Bluebird's feathers were a very dull ugly color. It lived near a lake with waters of the most delicate blue which never changed because no stream flowed in or out. Because the bird admired the blue water, it bathed in the lake four times every morning for four days, and every morning it sang:

> There's a blue water.
> It lies there.
> I went in.
> I am all blue.

On the fourth morning it shed all its feathers and came out in its bare skin, but on the fifth morning it came out with blue feathers.

All the while, Coyote had been watching the bird. He wanted to jump in and catch it for his dinner, but he was afraid of the blue water. But on the fifth morning he said to the Bluebird: "How is it that all your ugly color has come out of your feathers, and now you are all blue and sprightly and beautiful? You are more beautiful than anything that flies in the air. I want to be blue, too."

"I went in only four times," replied the Bluebird. It then taught Coyote the song it had sung.

And so Coyote steeled his courage and jumped into the lake. For four mornings he did this, singing the song the Bluebird had taught him, and on the fifth day he turned as blue as the bird.

That made Coyote feel very proud. He was so proud to be a blue coyote that when he walked along he looked about on every side to see if anyone was noticing how fine and blue he was.

Then he started running along very fast, looking at his shadow to see if it also was blue. He was not watching the road, and presently he ran into a stump so hard that it threw him down upon the ground and he became dust-colored all over. And to this day all coyotes are the color of dusty earth.

The Story of the Bat
(Creek)

The birds challenged the four-footed animals to play them in a ball game. Each group agreed that all creatures that had teeth should play on the side of the animals, and all those that had feathers should play on the side of the birds.

They chose a suitable day, cleared a playing field, erected poles, and obtained balls from the medicine men.

When the players gathered, all that had teeth went on one side and those that had feathers went on the other. When the Bat came, he joined the animals that had teeth.

"No," the animals said to Bat. "You have wings. You must play with the birds."

Bat went over to the side of the birds, but they said: "No, you have teeth. You must play with the animals." They drove him away, saying: "You are so small, you could do us no good anyway."

And so Bat went back to the animals, begging them to let him play with them. At last they agreed: "You are too small to help us, but as you have teeth we will let you remain on our side."

The game began, and the birds quickly took the lead because they could catch the ball in the air where the four-footed animals could not reach it. The Crane was the best player, and he caught the ball so often that it looked as if the birds were going to win the game. As none of the animals could fly, they were in despair.

The little bat now entered the game, flying into the air and catching the ball while the Crane was flapping slowly along. Again and again Bat caught the ball, and he won the game for the four-footed animals.

They agreed that even though Bat was very small and had wings he should always be classed with the animals having teeth.

Crow and Hawk
(Cochiti)

Crow had a nest in which she laid two eggs. For a day or so she sat on the eggs to hatch them, but then she grew tired of this and went off to hunt food for herself. Day after day passed but Crow did not return, and every morning Hawk flew by and saw the eggs with no one there to keep them warm.

One morning Hawk said to herself, "Crow who owns this nest no longer cares for it. Those eggs should not be lying unwarmed. I will sit on them and when they hatch they will be my children."

For many days Hawk sat on the eggs and Crow never came to the nest. Finally the eggs began to hatch. Still no Crow came. Both little ones hatched out and mother Hawk flew about getting food for them. They grew larger and larger until their wings became strong. Then mother Hawk took them off the nest and showed them how to fly.

About this time, Crow remembered her nest and she came back to it. She found the eggs hatched and Hawk taking care of her little ones. Hawk was on the ground, feeding with the young crows.

"Hawk, what do you think you are doing?" cried Crow.

"I am doing nothing wrong," Hawk said.

"You must return these young crows you are leading around."

"Why?"

"Because they are mine," Crow replied.

"To be sure, you laid the eggs," Hawk said, "but you went off and left them. There was no one to sit upon them and keep them warm. I came and sat upon the nest and hatched them. When they were hatched I fed them and now I am showing them how to find their own food. They are mine and I shall not return them to you."

"I shall take them back," Crow threatened.

"I shall not give them up. I have worked for them. Many days I went without food sitting there upon the eggs. In all that time you did not come near your nest. Why is it that now I have done all the work to hatch and raise them you want them back?"

Crow looked down at the young ones. "My children," she said, "come with me. I am your mother."

But the young ones answered: "We do not know you. Hawk is our mother."

At last, after she saw that she could not make the little crows come with her, Crow said: "Very well, I shall take this matter to Eagle, the King of the Birds, and let him decide. We shall see who has the right to these young crows."

"Good," said Hawk. "I am willing to go and tell the King of the Birds about this."

And so Crow and Hawk and the two young birds went to see Eagle. Crow spoke first. "When I returned to my nest," she said, "I found my eggs hatched and Hawk taking charge of my young ones. I have come to you, the King of the Birds, to ask that Hawk be required to return the children to me."

"Why did you leave your nest?" Eagle asked Crow.

To this question, Crow gave no reply. She simply bowed her head in silence.

"Very well, Hawk," Eagle said, "how did you find this nest of eggs?"

"Many times I flew over the nest and found it empty," Hawk replied. "No one came for a long time, and so I said to myself, 'The mother who made this nest can no longer care for these eggs. I shall be glad to hatch these little ones.' So I sat on the nest and warmed the eggs until they hatched. Then I went about getting food for the young ones. I worked hard and taught them to fly and to find food for themselves."

"But they are my children," Crow interrupted. "I laid the eggs."

Eagle glared at Crow. "Wait for your turn to speak," he said sternly, and then turned back to Hawk. "Is that all you have to say, Hawk?"

"Yes, I have worked hard to raise my two young ones. Just when they are able to care for themselves, Crow comes back and asks to have them given to her. It is I who went without food for days so as to stay on the nest and keep the eggs warm. The birds are now my little ones. I do not wish to give them up."

Eagle thought a few moments, muttering aloud to himself: "It seems that mother Hawk is not willing to return the young ones to mother Crow. If mother Crow had truly wanted these young ones, why did she leave the nest for so many days, and now is demanding that they be given to her? In truth, Hawk is the mother of the young ones because she went without food while she warmed and hatched them and then flew about searching out their food. So now they are her children."

When she heard this. Crow approached closer to Eagle. "Oh, King of the Birds," she said, "why do you not ask the young ones which mother they will choose to follow? They are old enough to know that they are crows and not hawks."

Eagle nodded his head and turned to the young ones. "Which mother will you choose?" he asked.

Both young Crows answered together: "Hawk is our mother. She is the only mother we know."

"No!" cried Crow. "I am your only mother!"

The young crows then said to her: "You abandoned us in the nest. Hawk hatched us and took care of us and she is our mother."

"It is settled," Eagle declared. "The young ones have chosen Hawk to be their mother. So it shall be."

At this, Crow began to weep.

"It is useless to weep," said Eagle. "You abandoned your nest and it is your own fault that you have lost your children. It is the decision of the King of the Birds that they shall go with mother Hawk."

And so the young crows stayed with Hawk, and Crow lost her children.

Why Coyote Stopped Imitating His Friends
(Caddo)

Coyote and Raven were good friends. One day after Coyote had grown weary of hunting for food and finding none, he decided to go to the top of Blue Mountain to see his friend Raven. "Welcome," Raven said. "But why do you look so weary and sad, my friend?"

"I have been hunting for food," replied Coyote, "but I found nothing."

Upon hearing this, Raven put an arrow to his bow and shot it straight up into the air, and then stood waiting for it to come down. It came down and pierced his upper wing. When Raven drew the arrow out, it had a large piece of buffalo meat fixed to the head. Raven gave the meat to Coyote, who smacked his mouth and ate heartily.

"That was a fine piece of meat," Coyote said. "I must repay you some time. Will you come and visit me soon?"

"Yes, I will come," promised Raven.

Coyote did not know that Raven possessed magic powers over the buffalo, and he believed that he could perform the same trick to obtain meat. In expectation of Raven's visit, he made himself a new bow, and a few days later Raven came down from Blue Mountain to see him.

"Welcome, welcome," Coyote greeted him. "I have no meat because I did not expect you, but if you will wait a moment I will soon have some for you."

Coyote took his new bow and shot an arrow straight up into the sky. He then stood waiting for it to come down. Raven watched him but said not a word. The arrow came down and struck Coyote's thigh. He ran away screaming with pain, leaving his guest behind. Raven waited a while and then went home without any meat, but in very high spirits because Coyote's attempt to imitate him amused him greatly. For days he chuckled to himself whenever he thought of it.

As for Coyote, he ran for miles until he finally had the sense to stop and pull the arrow out of his thigh. He was so humiliated that he broke the arrow to pieces, and then wandered off and hid in the woods.

After a time he grew hungry, and when he could find nothing to eat he decided to go up on Rich Mountain and visit Black Bear. "Welcome, old friend," said Black Bear. "I will see if I can get some food to offer you." As he spoke he leaned against a persimmon tree that was weighted down with ripe persimmons. His body jarred the tree so that the ripe fruit fell to the ground.

Bear smiled and asked his friend to eat. Coyote ate persimmons until he was no longer hungry, and then he filled his pack with them. "Thank you, indeed, my friend," said Coyote. "I must be going now, but I insist that you promise to visit me soon."

Next day Coyote wandered all about looking for a persimmon tree. He could not find one with any fruit on it, and so he cut down one without fruit. He carried it home where he set it up. Then he took the persimmons he had brought in his pack and tied them to the tree branches so that they looked as though they had grown there.

Not long after that, Black Bear came by to make his promised visit. "I am glad to see you," said Coyote. "Wait a moment and I will try to get you something to eat." Coyote began bumping against the persimmon tree with his head. He butted harder and harder but the persimmons were tied on so well they would not fall off. Finally he shook the tree with his paws, although it embarrassed him to have to do this. He gave the tree a big shake and over it fell, crashing upon his head. He pretended that it did not hurt and went about gathering up the fruit for Bear, but he could hardly see for the pain. The knot on his head kept growing larger and larger.

Bear ate, but he could scarcely swallow for laughing at the way Coyote had tried to imitate him. After a while he told Coyote that it was time for him to leave. He was afraid to stay longer for fear Coyote would see him laugh. After Bear left, Coyote sat down and held his sore head, but he felt happy because he had furnished food for his friend Black Bear.

A few days later while Coyote was out in the forest looking for something to eat, he came upon a grass lodge that he had never seen before. Wondering who might live in the new lodge and if they might have some food to share with him, he went right up to the entrance and called out: "Hello in there. I'm Coyote."

"And I'm Woodpecker," a voice replied. "Come in."

Coyote entered and saw a bird walking around with a bright

light on his head. "Say, friend," cried Coyote, "your head is on fire, and you and your house will burn up if you don't put it out."

The Red-Headed Woodpecker smiled and replied in a calm voice: "I've always worn this light on my head. It was given to me in the beginning. It will not burn anything." Woodpecker then gave Coyote something to eat.

After Coyote had eaten all he could, he arose and said that he must go. "Please come over and make me a visit," he said, "and I shall return your hospitality."

Some time later Woodpecker visited Coyote's lodge. "Is anybody home?" he called out at the entrance.

"Just a moment," replied Coyote. Woodpecker could hear him rustling around inside, and then Coyote said: "Now, come in and be seated."

Woodpecker entered and was surprised to see a bunch of burning straw on Coyote's head. "Oh, take that off," cried Woodpecker. "You will burn your head."

Coyote smiled and replied in a calm voice: "No, no, that will not burn my head. I always wear it. I was told in the beginning that I would wear a light on my head at nights so that I can do whatever I like while others are in darkness."

Coyote had no more than finished speaking when the hair on his head caught fire. He began to scream in pain and tried to put it out, but could not. He ran out of his lodge, howling all the way to the river. Woodpecker waited a long time for him to return, but Coyote stayed in the river all day trying to soothe his burned head.

After that, Coyote stopped trying to imitate his friends.

IX
Ghost Stories

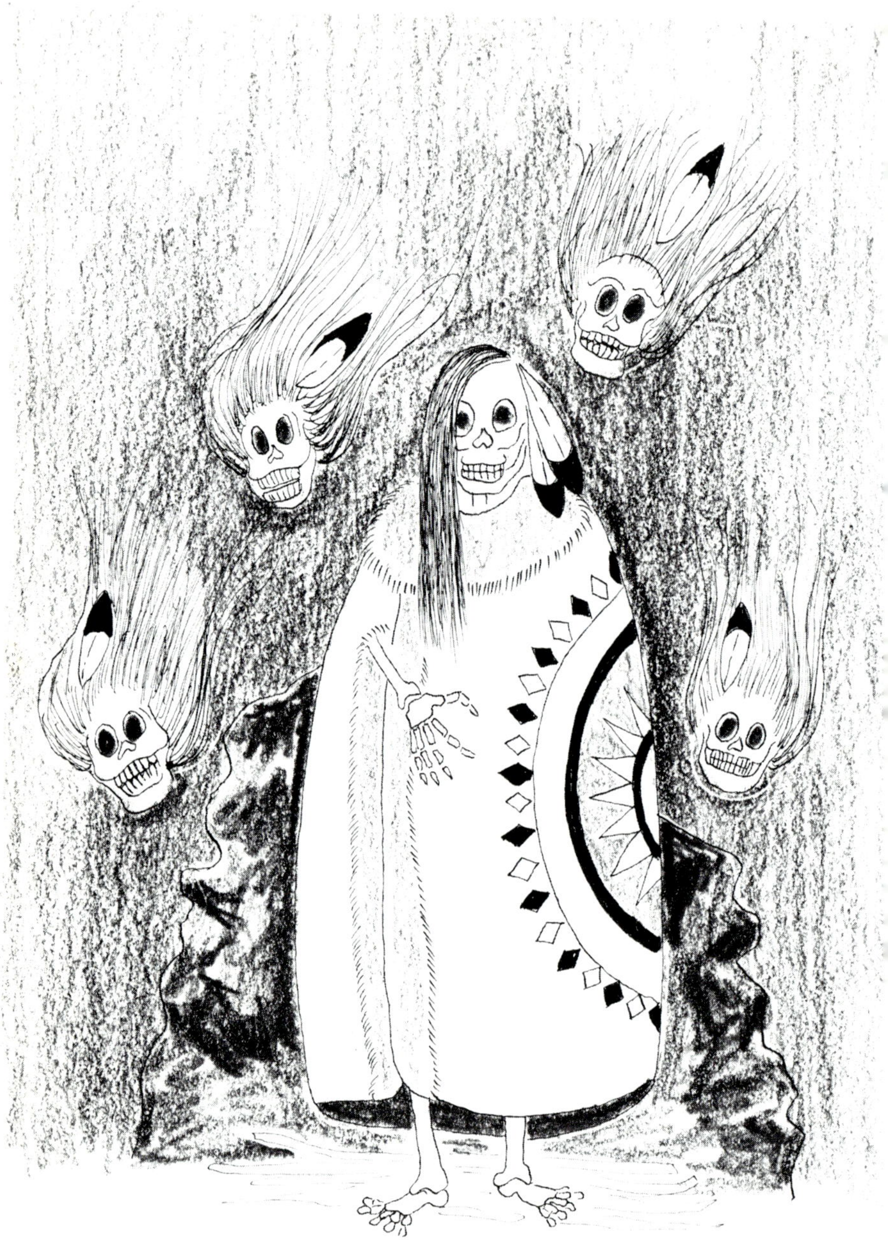

On cold winter nights when the wind howled and shrieked, story-tellers around the tepee fires usually had at least one tale to tell of ghosts that would send shivers tingling along the spines of their listeners. Instead of appearing as white wraiths, American Indian ghosts more often were skeletons, and they behaved in various ways. Sometimes they performed good deeds. At other times they were capricious, seeking to do harm in some way, or simply teasing and frightening those of the living who happened to cross their paths.

The Lame Warrior and the Skeleton
(Arapaho)

In the days before horses, a party of young Arapahos set off on foot one autumn morning in search of wild game in the western mountains. They carried heavy packs of food and spare moccasins, and one day as they were crossing the rocky bed of a shallow stream a young warrior felt a sudden sharp pain in his ankle. The ankle swelled and the pain grew worse until they pitched camp that night.

Next morning the warrior's ankle was swollen so badly that it was impossible for him to continue the journey with the others. His companions decided it was best to leave him. They cut young willows and tall grass to make a thatched shelter for him, and after the shelter was finished they collected a pile of dry wood so that he could keep a fire burning.

"When your ankle gets well," they told him, "don't try to follow us. Go back to our village, and await our return."

After several lonely days, the lame warrior tested his ankle, but it was still too painful to walk upon. And then one night a heavy snowstorm fell, virtually imprisoning him in the shelter. Because he had been unable to kill any wild game, his food supply was almost gone.

Late one afternoon he looked out and saw a large herd of buffalo rooting in the snow for grass quite close to his shelter. Reaching for his bow and arrow, he shot the fattest one and killed it. He then crawled out of the shelter to the buffalo, skinned it, and brought in the meat. After preparing a bed of coals, he placed a section of ribs in the fire for roasting.

Night had fallen by the time the ribs were cooked, and just as the lame warrior was reaching for a piece to eat, he heard footsteps crunching on the frozen snow. The steps came nearer and nearer to the closed flap of the shelter. "Who can that be?" he said to himself. "I am here alone and unable to run, but I shall defend myself if need be." He reached for his bow and arrow.

A moment later the flap opened and a skeleton clothed in a tanned robe stood there looking down at the lame warrior.

The robe was pinned tight at the neck so that only the skull was visible above and skeleton feet below. Frightened by this ghost, the warrior turned his eyes away from it.

"You must not be frightened of me," the skeleton said in a hoarse voice. "I have taken pity on you. Now you must take pity on me. Give me a piece of those roast ribs to eat, for I am very hungry."

Still very much alarmed by the presence of this unexpected visitor, the warrior offered a large piece of meat to an extended bony hand. He was astonished to see the skeleton chew the food with its bared teeth and swallow it.

"It was I who gave you the pain in your ankle," said the skeleton. "It was I who caused your ankle to swell so that you could not continue on the hunt. If you had gone on with your companions you would have been killed. The day they left you here, an enemy war party made a charge upon them, and they were all killed. I am the one who saved your life."

Again the skeleton's bony hand reached out, this time to rub the warrior's ankle. The pain and swelling vanished at once. "Now you can walk again," the ghost said. "Your enemies are all around, but if you will follow me I can lead you safely back to your village."

At dawn they left the shelter and started off across the snow, the skeleton leading the way. They walked through deep woods, along icy streams, and over high hills. Late in the afternoon the skeleton led the warrior up a steep ridge. When the warrior reached the summit, the ghost had vanished, but down in the valley below he could see the smokes of tepees in his Arapaho village.

Heavy Collar and the Ghost Woman
(Blackfoot)

One summer while the Blackfeet were camped on Old Man's River, a chief named Heavy Collar chose seven young warriors to go with him on a buffalo hunt. They traveled around the Cypress Mountains, but found no buffalo and started back toward their camp. On the way Heavy Collar took the lead, for they had found signs of large enemy war parties and he wanted to keep his small group moving in the concealment of coulees and other low places as much as possible.

One afternoon as Heavy Collar was leading the way up a wide river, he sighted three old buffalo bulls lying close to a steep bank. He ran along at a fast trot, circling through a dry gulch so as to come close to the buffalo. He killed one with an arrow and butchered it. As he was hungry, he took a piece of meat down into the gulch and built a smokeless fire to roast it. Before his seven young warriors could find him, night came on very rapidly. "Perhaps I should have waited for my young men," he said aloud, "but I feared the buffalo would run away. Before it is completely dark I should climb up on the bank and try to signal them. I could also get some hair from that buffalo's head and wipe out my gun."

While he sat there thinking of these things and talking to himself, a ball of buffalo hair came floating to him through the air, falling on the ground right in front of him. When this happened, it startled him a little because he thought enemies might have trapped him alone and thrown the ball of hair at him. After a while he picked up the hair and cleaned his gun with it. He reloaded the weapon and then sat watching and listening as darkness deepened. He was very uneasy and decided to go farther up the riverbank to scout out the country. When he came to the mouth of St. Mary's River, it was very late in the night. He was so tired that he crept into a patch of high rye-grass to hide and sleep.

Now Heavy Collar did not know that he had come to a camp

ground where another tribe of Indians had lived the summer before. Those Indians had been surprised by a war party. A woman had been killed during the fight, and her body was left behind in the very patch of rye-grass where Heavy Collar had lain down to rest. Although he was very tired, Heavy Collar could not sleep. He thought that he could hear sounds of movement, but what it was he could not make out. Every time he dozed off he thought he heard something nearby. He spent the night there, and as soon as daylight came he saw a skeleton lying close beside him. It was the skeleton of the woman who had been killed the previous summer.

Troubled by fears, Heavy Collar started on to the buttes beyond Belly River, a hilly place where he and his warriors had arranged to meet in case any of them became separated from the others. All day he kept thinking about his having slept beside an unknown woman's bones, and this made him more and more uneasy. He could not put it out of his mind. By day's end he was very tired because he had slept so little during the night. About sundown he crossed the river shallows to an island and decided to camp there for the night.

At the upper end of the island he found a fallen tree that had drifted downstream and lodged there. Using the tree fork as a wind shelter, he built a fire, and then sat on one of the limbs with his back to the blaze, warming himself. All the time he kept thinking about the skeleton he had slept beside the previous night. As he sat there, he heard a sudden sound behind him, a sound of something being dragged across the ground toward the fire. It was like the sound of a tepee cover being pulled across the grass. It came closer and closer.

Heavy Collar was more frightened than he had been in a long time. He was so afraid that he could not turn his head to look back and see what was making the noise. The dragging sound seemed to come up to the fallen tree where his fire was burning. Then it stopped, and suddenly he heard someone whistling a tune.

He turned around then and looked toward the sound, and there, sitting on the other fork of the tree, facing him, was the same skeleton beside which he had slept the night before. This ghost was now wearing a piece of old tepee cover. The tepee cover had a lodgepole string tied to it, and this string was fastened about the ghost's neck. The wings of the tepee cover appeared to stretch out and fade away into the darkness. The ghost began whistling a tune, and as it whistled, it swung its legs to the tune.

When Heavy Collar saw this strange sight, his heart almost stopped beating. Finally he gathered enough courage to speak: "Oh ghost, go away and do not trouble me. I am very tired. I want to rest and sleep."

But his words only made the ghost whistle louder, and swing its legs more violently. The skull turned from side to side, sometimes looking down upon him, sometimes looking at the stars in the sky, but always whistling.

When Heavy Collar saw that the ghost was paying no heed to his pleas, he grew angry and said: "Well, ghost, you do not take pity upon me, and so I shall have to shoot you and drive you away." He picked up his gun and fired point-blank at the ghost. It fell over backward into the darkness, crying out: "You have shot me, Heavy Collar, you have killed me! You are no better than a dog, Heavy Collar. I curse you. There is no place on earth you can go that I will not find you, no place you can hide that I will not come."

At this, Heavy Collar jumped to his feet and ran away as fast as he could. Behind him he could hear the voice of the ghost calling in the night: "I have been killed once, Heavy Collar, and now you are trying to kill me again." The words followed him until at last they died away in the distance. He ran and ran through the darkness, and whenever he stopped to catch his breath he could hear far away the sound of his name being repeated again and again in a mournful voice. He was very sleepy, but dared not lie down, for he remembered the ghost's threat to follow him wherever he went. At first daylight he sat down to rest, and at once fell asleep.

In the meantime Heavy Collar's party of seven young warriors had gone on to the rendezvous point in the buttes beyond Belly River to await their leader's arrival. On that morning one of the young men, who was posted on a high hill to watch for Heavy

Collar, saw two persons approaching. As they came nearer, the warrior saw that one of them was Heavy Collar. The other was a woman. The watcher called out to the others in the party: "Here comes our chief! He is bringing a woman with him." They all laughed, and joked about how they would take her away from him.

When the two persons reached the top of a level ridge, Heavy Collar began walking very fast. The woman would walk by his side for a few steps; then she would fall behind and would have to trot along to catch up with him again. Immediately in front of the young warriors' camp was a deep coulee through which the chief and the woman had to cross. The warriors saw them go down into the coulee side by side, but when Heavy Collar walked out of it, he was alone. He shouted a greeting to the young men, and strode on into their camp.

"Heavy Collar," one of them called out, "where is your woman?"

The chief frowned at them for a moment. "I have no woman," he said. They laughed at him then, and he added: "I don't understand what you're talking about."

One of them said: "Our chief must have hidden her in that coulee."

Another asked: "Where did you capture her, and of what tribe is she?"

Heavy Collar looked from one young man to another, and said: "I think you are all crazy. I have captured no woman. What do you mean?"

One warrior replied: "Why, we all saw you walking with that woman when you went down into the coulee. Where did she come from, and where did you leave her? Is she down in the coulee? We saw her and it's no use to deny that she was with you."

By this time Heavy Collar knew that the woman they had seen must have been the ghost that had been following him. He sat down and told them what had happened the previous night. Some of the warriors refused to believe him. They ran down to the coulee where they had last seen the woman, and although they found the prints of Heavy Collar's moccasins, there were no other tracks near his.

Now they believed that the woman was indeed a ghost, but there was no sign of her that night. The next morning they started on the return journey to the Blackfoot camp on Old Man's River. Darkness had fallen before they reached the camp, and their friends and relatives invited them to feast with them.

After the celebration, Heavy Collar sat for a while in front of his tepee enjoying the peaceful moonlit night. Suddenly a noise sounded in the brush, and he was relieved to see that it was only a bear coming out of the woods. He felt around for a stone to throw at the bear to frighten it away. Finding a piece of bone, he threw it at the bear, hitting it a sharp blow.

"Well, well, well, Heavy Collar," said the bear. "You have killed me once, and now you are hitting me. I told you there was no place in the world where you can hide from me. I don't care where you may go, I will always find you."

Knowing that this was the ghost woman who had taken the shape of a bear, Heavy Collar ran for his tepee entrance, shouting as loud as he could: "Run, run! A ghost bear is upon us!"

Everyone in camp came running toward Heavy Collar's tepee, and in a few minutes it was crowded with people. A big fire was burning below the smoke-hole, and a hard wind from the west was shaking the tepee. Men, women, and children huddled together in fear of the ghost they had been told about. Outside they could hear the ghost's footsteps walking toward the lodge. "These people are no better than dogs," the ghost cried. "I will kill them all. Not one of them shall escape." The sounds kept coming closer and closer until they seemed to be right outside the closed entrance. Then the ghost said: "I will smoke you to death." As it said this, it moved the poles so that the wings of the tepee turned toward the west and the wind could blow in freely through the smoke-hole.

As the tepee began to fill with smoke, the ghost continued making terrible threats. Children began crying, and everyone was weeping and coughing from the suffocating smoke.

"Let's lift a man up to fix the tepee ears," Heavy Collar said, "so my lodge will get clear of smoke." They raised a man on their shoulders, but he was so blinded and strangled by the smoke that he had difficulty in turning the wings. While he was doing this, the ghost suddenly struck the tepee a hard blow, frightening those who were holding the man on their shoulders so that they let him fall down. "It's no use," said Heavy Collar. "That ghost woman is determined to smoke us to death." By this time the smoke was so thick in the tepee that they could barely see each other.

"Is there no one here who has strong enough power to overcome this ghost?" Heavy Collar called out in desperation.

"I am the oldest of the tribe," his mother replied. "I will try." She quickly found her medicine bundle and painted herself. Then she lighted her dead husband's pipe and thrust the stem out through a crack in the entrance cover. "Oh, ghost," she said in a quavering voice, "smoke this pipe and go away."

"No, no, no," the ghost answered. "You people are dogs. I will not listen to you. Every one of you must die."

"Ghost, take pity upon us," the old woman repeated. "Smoke this pipe and go away in peace."

Then the ghost said: "How can you expect me to smoke when I am outside the tepee. Bring the pipe to me. I have no long bill like a bird with which to reach the stem."

The old woman lifted the entrance cover and stepped outside. With her feeble hand she extended the pipe toward the sound of the ghost's voice.

"Bring the pipe closer," the ghost commanded. "If you want me to smoke it, you must bring it to me."

Again the old woman went toward the ghost, which backed away, saying angrily: "No, I don't wish to smoke that kind of pipe." As it spoke, the ghost moved farther away and the old woman felt herself being pulled after it by some powerful force. She cried out in fear: "Oh, my children, the ghost is carrying me off!"

As Heavy Collar rushed to help her, he called to the others: "Come and help me save my mother from the ghost." He grasped his mother by the waist and held her until another man caught him by the waist. All the others then came out of the tepee until they were in a long line, pulling on each other with all their might. No matter how hard they pulled, however, the ghost drew them slowly towards it.

And then all of a sudden the old woman turned loose the pipe and fell down dead upon the ground. At the same instant the ghost disappeared. After that, Heavy Collar was never troubled by the ghost woman. Nor was the pipe ever seen again.

The Sioux Who Wrestled With A Ghost
(Sioux)

A young Sioux warrior went out alone to live with the animals and birds for a time. He was seeking a vision from Wakantanka, the Great Mystery, so that he would know what direction to take in life. After meeting and overcoming many difficulties he reached a wilderness. One day as he was walking along through a forest he heard a voice. He searched all around, but could find nothing but an owl sitting in a tree.

When night came on, he made a fire and sat down to warm himself. Suddenly he heard the voice again, singing very loudly. The Sioux shouted to the singer, but no one replied, and after a while the sound died away.

The only food the Sioux had was a small pouch of *wasna*, or buffalo fat mixed with dried meat and wild cherries. He was reaching for the pouch when the sound of singing came again, even louder than before, and when the Sioux looked up he saw a ghost standing on the edge of the firelight.

"I want some of your food," the ghost said.

"I have nothing whatever," the young warrior replied.

"Not so," said the ghost. "I know that you have some *wasna*."

"All right. I will share it with you."

After they had eaten some of the *wasna*, the Sioux filled his pipe with tobacco and offered it to the ghost. When the ghost reached for the stem, the young man saw that the hand had no flesh, being nothing but bones. At the same time the ghost's robe dropped from its shoulders to its waist so that all its ribs were visible, there being no flesh on them. Although the ghost did not open its teeth as it smoked, the smoke was pouring out through its ribs.

When it had finished smoking, the ghost said to the Sioux: "We must wrestle each other. If you can throw me, I will make you rich in horses."

As the young man owned no horses, he agreed to wrestle the ghost, but before beginning he gathered a pile of brush for his fire so as to light up the forest. While he was doing this the ghost rushed upon him, seizing him with its bony hands and squeezing him most painfully. He tried to push the ghost away, but its legs were very powerful.

After a time, the Sioux noticed that when they wrestled near the fire, the ghost became weak, but the farther they moved away from the fire the stronger the ghost became. As the fire burned lower and lower, the strength of the ghost increased. The young man struggled harder, but the ghost's bones grew tighter around him. After a desperate effort he managed to get near enough to the fire to kick a piece of dry wood into the coals.

As soon as the fire blazed up, the ghost fell upon the ground as though it were coming to pieces. "You have won," the ghost said hoarsely. "Now follow me."

Just as dawn was breaking, the ghost led the Sioux out through the woods into a valley filled with hundreds of horses. The young man roped as many as he could lead back to his village. He never saw the ghost again, but after that he believed in ghosts and whatever they might have to say to people.

SOURCES

I WHEN ANIMALS LIVED AS EQUALS WITH THE PEOPLE

THE ROOSTER, THE MOCKINGBIRD AND THE MAIDEN (Hopi)
Told by Kiwanhongva of Oraibi to H. R. Voth about 1903.
Voth, H. R. *Traditions of the Hopi* (Field Columbian Museum, Publication 96, Pp. 176–179). Chicago 1905.

THE BEAR MAN (Cherokee)
Told by John Ax to James Mooney in the 1880s.
Mooney, James *Myths of the Cherokee* (U.S. Bureau of American Ethnology, 19th Annual Report, Pp. 327–329). Washington 1898.

HOW ANTELOPE CARRIER SAVED THE THUNDERBIRDS (Arikara)
Told by Antelope of the Arikaras to George A. Dorsey in 1903.
Dorsey, George A. *Traditions of the Arikara*, Pp. 73–78. Carnegie Institution, Washington 1904.

WHY DOGS HAVE LONG TONGUES (Caddo)
Told by Hinie of the Caddos to George A. Dorsey in 1903.
Dorsey, George A. *Traditions of the Caddo*, Pp. 82–83. Carnegie Institution, Washington 1905.

THE GREAT SHELL OF KINTYEL (Navaho)
From a rite-myth told by Tall Chanter of the Navahos to Washington Matthews in the 1890s.
Matthews, Washington *Navaho Legends*, Pp. 195–208. Published for the American Folklore Society by Houghton, Mifflin and Company, Boston 1897.

THE GIRL WHO CLIMBED TO THE SKY (Arapaho-Caddo)
From stories told by Annie Wilson and Wing of the Caddos to George A. Dorsey in 1904, and by Long Hair and other Arapahos to Alfred L. Kroeber about 1902.
Dorsey, George A. *Traditions of the Caddo*, Pp. 82–83. Carnegie Institution, Washington 1905; Dorsey, George A. and Kroeber, Alfred L. *Traditions of the Arapaho* (Field Columbian Museum, Publication 81, Pp. 330–341). Chicago 1903.

II BEFORE THE WHITE MEN CAME
THE CHEYENNE PROPHET (Cheyenne)
From stories collected among the Cheyennes by George A. Dorsey (1901) and George B. Grinnell (1907).
Grinnell, George B. "Some Early Cheyenne Tales", *Journal of American Folklore*, Vol. XXI, Pp. 271-303. 1908; Dorsey, George A. *The Cheyenne* (Field Columbian Museum, Publication 99, Pp. 1-55). Chicago 1905.

THE DEEDS AND PROPHECIES OF OLD MAN (Blackfoot)
From stories collected among the Blackfoot by George B. Grinnell (1892) and Clark Wissler (1908).
Grinnell, George B. *Blackfoot Lodge Tales*, Pp. 137-144. Charles Scribner's Sons, New York 1892; Wissler, Clark and Duvall, D. C. *Mythology of the Blackfoot Indians* (American Museum of Natural History, Anthropological Paper, Vol. II, Part One, Pp. 19-21). New York 1908.

HOW DAY AND NIGHT WERE DIVIDED (Creek)
From a story collected from the Creeks by William O. Tuggle in the 1880s.
Swanton, John R. *Myths and Tales of the Southeastern Indians* (U.S. Bureau of American Ethnology, Bulletin 88, P.2). Washington 1929.

HOW THE BUFFALO WERE RELEASED ON EARTH (Apache-Comanche)
Told by White Mountain Apaches to P. E. Goddard in 1919 and by Comanches to H. H. St. Clair in 1909.
Goddard, Pliny Earle *White Mountain Apache Myths and Tales* (American Museum of Natural History, Anthropological Papers, Vol. XXIV, Pp. 126-127). New York 1919; St. Clair, H. H. and Lowie, R. H. "Shoshone and Comanche Tales", *Journal of American Folklore*, Vol. XXII, Pp. 280-281. 1909.

HOW CORN CAME TO EARTH (Arikara)
Told by Hand of the Arikaras to George A. Dorsey in 1903.
Dorsey, George A. *Traditions of the Arikara*, Pp. 12-17. Carnegie Institution, Washington 1904.

HOW RABBIT BROUGHT FIRE TO THE PEOPLE (Creek)
From stories collected among the Creeks by William O. Tuggle in the 1880s and by John R. Swanton about 1908.
Swanton, John R. *Myths and Tales of the Southeastern Indians* (U.S. Bureau of American Ethnology, Bulletin 88, Pp. 46, 102-103). Washington 1929.

GODASIYO THE WOMAN CHIEF (Seneca)
Told by an unidentified Seneca on Cattaraugus Reservation, New York, to J. N. B. Hewitt in 1896.
Curtin, Jeremiah and Hewitt, J. N. B. *Seneca Fiction, Legends and Myths* (U.S. Bureau of American Ethnology, 32nd Annual Report 1910–1911, Pp. 537–538). Government Printing Office, Washington 1918.

III ALLEGORIES
THE RETURN OF ICE MAN (Cherokee)
Told by Swimmer of the Cherokees to James Mooney in the 1880s.
Mooney, James *Myths of the Cherokees* (U.S. Bureau of American Ethnology, 19th Annual Report, Pp. 322–323). Washington 1898.

ICE MAN AND THE MESSENGER OF SPRINGTIME (Chippewa)
Told by an unidentified Chippewa to Henry R. Schoolcraft early in the 19th century.
Schoolcraft, Henry R. *The Myth of Hiawatha*, Pp. 96–97. J. B. Lippincott & Company, Philadelphia 1856.

IV FIRST CONTACTS WITH EUROPEANS
HOW IOSCODA AND HIS FRIENDS MET THE WHITE MEN (Ottawa)
Told by the Ottawas to Henry R. Schoolcraft early in the 19th century.
Schoolcraft, Henry R. *The Myth of Hiawatha*, Pp. 278–291. J. B. Lippincott & Company, Philadelphia 1856.

KATLIAN AND THE IRON PEOPLE (Tlingit)
Told by Richard of the Tlingits to John R. Swanton about 1904.
Swanton, John R. *Haida Texts and Myths* (U.S. Bureau of American Ethnology, Bulletin 29). Government Printing Office, Washington 1905.

HOW THE FIRST WHITE MEN CAME TO THE CHEYENNES (Cheyenne)
Told by Black Pipe of the Cheyennes to Lieutenant William P. Clark in the 1870s.
Clark, William P. *Indian Sign Language*, Pp. 104–105. L. R. Hamersley & Company, 1885.

V THE COMING OF THE HORSE
HOW A PIEGAN WARRIOR FOUND THE FIRST HORSES (Blackfoot)
Told by Almost-a-Dog of the Piegan Blackfoot to George B. Grinnell late in the 19th century.

Grinnell, George B. *The Story of the Indian*, Pp. 166–168. D. Appleton & Company, New York 1896.

WATER SPIRIT'S GIFT OF HORSES (Blackfoot)
Told by Chewing-Back-Bones of the Blackfoot to John C. Ewers in 1943.
Ewers, John C. *The Horse in Blackfoot Indian Culture* (U.S. Bureau of American Ethnology, Bulletin 159, Pp. 294–295). Government Printing Office, Washington 1955.

VI TRICKSTERS AND MAGICIANS

HOW RABBIT FOOLED WOLF (Creek)
Told by the Creeks to John R. Swanton about 1908.
Swanton, John R. *Myths of the Southeastern Indians* (U.S. Bureau of American Ethnology, Bulletin 88, Pp. 63–66). Government Printing Office, Washington 1929.

COYOTE AND THE ROLLING ROCK (Salish-Blackfoot)
Told by the Salish, or Flatheads, to Louisa McDermott about 1900, by the Blackfoot to George B. Grinnell about 1890, and by the Blackfoot to D. C. Duvall between 1903 and 1907.
McDermott, Louisa "Folklore of the Flathead Indians of Idaho", *Journal of American Folklore*, Vol. XIV, Pp. 240–251. 1901; Grinnell, George B. *Blackfoot Lodge Tales*, Pp. 165–166. Charles Scribner's Sons, New York 1892; Wissler, Clark and Duvall, D. C. *Mythology of the Blackfoot Indians* (American Museum of Natural History, Anthropological Papers, Vol. II, Part One, Pp. 24–25). New York 1908.

SKUNK OUTWITS COYOTE (Comanche)
Told by the Comanches to Harry H. St. Clair II, and edited by Robert Lowie in 1909.
Lowie, Robert H. and St. Clair II, Harry H. "Shoshone and Comanche Tales", *Journal of American Folklore*, Vol. XXII, Pp. 273–275. 1909.

NIHANCAN AND THE DWARF'S ARROW (Arapaho)
Told by the Arapahos to Alfred L. Kroeber about 1902.
Dorsey, George A. and Kroeber, Alfred L. *Traditions of the Arapaho* (Field Columbian Museum, Publication 81, Pp. 54–55). Chicago 1903.

SWIFT-RUNNER AND THE TRICKSTER TARANTULA (Zuni)
Told by the Zunis to Frank Hamilton Cushing late in the 19th century.
Cushing, Frank Hamilton *Zuni Folk Tales*, Pp. 345–364. G. P. Putnam's Sons, New York 1901.

BUFFALO WOMAN, A STORY OF MAGIC (Caddo)
Told by White-Bread of the Caddos to George A. Dorsey in 1903.
Dorsey, George A. *Traditions of the Caddo*, Pp. 73–76. Carnegie Institution, Washington 1905.

VII HEROES AND HEROINES

THE HUNTER AND THE DAKWA (Cherokee)
Told by Swimmer and Tagwadihi of the Cherokees to James Mooney in the 1880s.
Mooney, James *Myths of the Cherokee* (U.S. Bureau of American Ethnology, 19th Annual Report, Pp. 320–321). Washington 1898.

THE PRISONERS OF COURT HOUSE ROCK (Pawnee)
Told by the Pawnees to George B. Grinnell during the 1880s.
Grinnell, George B. *Pawnee Hero Stories and Folktales*, Pp. 67–69. Field and Stream Publishing Company, New York 1889.

RED SHIELD AND RUNNING WOLF (Crow)
Based in part upon a story collected on the Crow reservation in Montana by Robert H. Lowie about 1910.
Lowie, Robert H. *Myths and Traditions of the Crow Indians* (American Museum of Natural History, Anthropological Papers, Vol. XXV, Part One, Pp. 136–140). New York 1918.

VIII ANIMAL STORIES

THE BLUEBIRD AND THE COYOTE (Pima)
From a story collected from the Pima Indians by Frank Russell about 1905.
Russell, Frank *The Pima Indians* (U.S. Bureau of American Ethnology, 26th Annual Report, Pp. 245–246). 1904–1905.

THE STORY OF THE BAT (Creek)
Told by the Creeks to W. O. Tuggle in the 1880s.
Swanton, John R. *Myths of the Southeastern Indians* (U.S. Bureau of American Ethnology, Bulletin 88, P.23). Government Printing Office, Washington 1929.

CROW AND HAWK (Cochiti)
Told by a Cochiti woman to Ruth Benedict in 1924.
Benedict, Ruth *Tales of the Cochiti Indians* (U.S. Bureau of American Ethnology, Bulletin 98, Pp. 133–136. Government Printing Office, Washington 1931.

WHY COYOTE STOPPED IMITATING HIS FRIENDS (Caddo)
Told by Wing of the Caddos to George A. Dorsey in 1903.
Dorsey, George A. *Traditions of the Caddo*, Pp. 93–95. Carnegie Institution, Washington 1905.

IX GHOST STORIES

THE LAME WARRIOR AND THE SKELETON (Arapaho)
Told by Little Chief of the Southern Arapahos to George A. Dorsey about 1902.
Dorsey, George A. and Kroeber, Alfred L. *Traditions of the Arapaho* (Field Columbian Museum, Publication 81, Pp. 259–260). Chicago 1903.

HEAVY COLLAR AND THE GHOST WOMAN (Blackfoot)
Told by the Blackfoot to George B. Grinnell in the 1890s.
Grinnell, George B. *Blackfoot Lodge Tales*, Pp. 70–77. Charles Scribner's Sons, New York 1892.

THE SIOUX WHO WRESTLED WITH A GHOST (Sioux)
From a story recorded by George Bushotter of the Teton Sioux in 1888.
Dorsey, J. Owen *A Study of Siouan Cults* (U.S. Bureau of American Ethnology, 11th Annual Report, Pp. 490–491). Government Printing Office, Washington 1894.